AN ENGLISH
VINEYARD
COOKBOOK

AN ENGLISH
VINEYARD
COOKBOOK

Seasons, Recipes, Wines & Art

Peter Gladwin

Photographs by Ed Dallimore

LIST OF RECIPES

INTRODUCTION

The vineyard is like a family – full of trials and challenges and moments of great joy and fulfilment throughout the year. It has a life cycle of its own: the dormant vines burst forth in the spring; careful nurturing through the summer produces the best possible fruit; autumn is about harvesting, grape pressing and fermenting; and then the emerging wine must be matured, tasted, blended and bottled through the winter.

Bridget and I moved to West Sussex in 1991 to give our three wild sons a rural upbringing in the beautiful setting of vines, woodland, lakes and countryside. Nutbourne Vineyards became our home – a place to gather, grow, play, cook, eat and drink together as only a family can. More than 30 years on we are still enjoying the results of this lifestyle choice.

Let me introduce the family.

My wife, Bridget, is a talented artist, a highly accomplished cook, a natural grower and a fine mother. She has coped with four men in her life by balancing her strong will with a good sense of humour.

Richard is our eldest son – inspired, engaging and ever optimistic. He heads up The Gladwin Brothers Restaurant Group, operating five restaurants across London alongside his brother, Oliver.

Oliver is the chef. He is creative, skilled, outrageous and full of enthusiasm for all things edible, from foraging in the wild to whole animal butchery. He also presents cookery master classes to his peers in London.

The youngest is Gregory – a man of the countryside, a farmer and a winemaker. Highly able among his cows, pigs, sheep, tractors and vines, he is never keen to stray into a local town, let alone visit the metropolis.

My own working life has been in the world of food, drink and hospitality. I too am a chef, having run my own event catering company, restaurants and wine businesses, as well as writing about cookery, in a career of more than 50 years.

As you will see in some of the images in this book, each of our sons now has a family of his own — the next generation of culinary explorers.

Finally, Nutbourne has a wider family of other team members who work within this all-consuming rural environment. We all share a passion for wine, cooking and the glorious place where we are lucky enough to live and work.

The Gladwin Family together creates recipes for each season. We champion ingredients for every month, unashamedly using prime natural produce as often as we can. We grow fruits and vegetables, rear our own livestock, forage in the countryside and have a network of other growers, farmers and rural producers from whom we source the very best each season has to offer. Our cookery book aims to capture the natural wonders of the countryside and the occasions when we gather and celebrate. The recipes range from 'dead easy' family favourites to more sophisticated dishes we serve in our restaurants, but we have been careful to avoid techniques that cannot easily be accomplished at home.

Richard and Oliver bring their 'farm to fork' upbringing to their restaurants in residential areas of London under the collective title of Local & Wild – 'local produce and people, wild food and ideas'. They focus on all things Sussex. Of course, we lead with our own wines and produce from the farm, but also specialist produce from many other local growers and foraged ingredients from the countryside and coastline. Early in his career Oliver trained and cooked with the very best, including a long stint at River Cottage with Hugh Fearnley-Whittingstall. Oliver's cooking combines amazing flavours, textures and colours in delicious, often unexpected dishes, many of which we have featured in this book. He also shares some of his exciting and sometimes eccentric foraging tales.

What about the vineyard? English viticulture has come of age. There are some terrific people involved and some truly excellent wines, which only get better every year. Grape growing in the UK is a highly sustainable crop, the wines are fashionable and the magic associated with winemaking is ever present.

At Nutbourne every aspect of wine production takes place on the estate using our regenerative farming approach and artisan winemaking operation. From planting, nurturing and harvesting to pressing, fermenting and blending, we are going to share with you what is happening each month of the year and how we make sure our activities are climate positive. We annually produce between 40,000 and 80,000 bottles of still and sparkling wine. It is sold from our cellar door and restaurants but also distributed through a wide range of independent and like-minded merchants. The vineyard itself is open to visitors for 12 months of the year. Guests come to discover English wine, exploring, tasting and sharing the magic of this unique corner of Sussex.

Art and wine are linked throughout the world, each enhanced by the other. The secret to making great wine is as much art as science, and here at Nutbourne we have a direct family link. I have introduced Bridget as an artist. She paints in oils or acrylics on canvas and usually focuses on a particular subject matter for up to 18 months, creating a major body of work around a single theme. This can vary from the landscape of the South Downs, still life or transpositions of Old Masters to paintings of the vines themselves. Every label on a Nutbourne wine features a painting or a section of a canvas to complement the wine we have created. Our winery exhibits full-scale originals of some of Bridget's work both inside and, in summertime, on the walls outside.

As wine producers, we have friendships and great respect with other winemakers around the globe; we all learn and benefit from one another. In every section of the book we offer you our suggestions for a wide international range of wines to accompany our recipes. We invite you to dip into this cookbook for seasonal culinary inspiration, champion ingredients, foraging advice, wines and new recipe ideas. Alternatively we hope some readers may choose to read the book from cover to cover, skipping through the recipe details but enjoying the stories and insight into an English vineyard and family lifestyle.

At the end of the day there is something very special about drinking a wine made from your own grapes, grown and pressed in your own backyard; admiring a painting on a label when you know the artist; cooking vegetables and herbs from your own veg patch; eating steak from your own hand-reared cattle or gathering wild berries from the hedgerows around home. We value and enjoy the wonderful environment of the vineyard and Sussex countryside and are pleased to now share this with you through this book.

Peter Gladwin

SPRING

What a wonderful time of year to start a cookbook – daffodils swaying in the breeze, primrose-covered banks, the scent of wild garlic in the lanes, birds calling from the woodlands, each day staying light a little longer and new life emerging wherever we look. For me, spring is a time of new beginnings and new promise – our glorious countryside is coming back to life with all the intent of delivering a fabulous natural year.

THE VINEYARD

Throughout the winter the vineyard has been dormant, but now it starts to bud and then sprout new shoots. Luckily vines are usually slow starters, which is exactly what we want. One of the biggest threats to the grape crop is an early budburst in March followed by late frosts in April or May. Frost will destroy any open buds in a single night, devastating the potential for the whole year.

Nevertheless, the vines will burst into life every spring. Initially, lime-green shoots appear; these grow at an unbelievable pace, inches each day as the ambitious plants search for more sunlight to fulfil their destiny. It is almost as though the vines know about the fine wine we are after and the accolades they can win if they perform well. The great saying among winemakers is that good wine is made in the vineyard – while what happens in the winery is down to the skill of the winemaker, no one can ever transform disappointing grapes into fine wine.

As soon as the growing season begins our team are busy working in the vines every day, rubbing off buds that appear in the wrong places and selecting the shoots with even spacing, being careful not to be too greedy but equally not reducing the potential for a high yield. As the spring progresses the vine must be tucked and trained to grow correctly through the trellis system, creating a fruiting zone with a leafy canopy above.

Throughout this period, we continue to face the threat of frost damage. We set up frost barriers and remain on alert to switch on giant fans to move the air. We don't use the 'bougie' burners at Nutbourne because of their environmental impact, but many French and British growers stay up all night when there is a frost risk, lighting thousands of these hot candles to preserve their crops.

The risk of frost slowly retreats, the vines grow stronger and the season progresses.

THE WINERY

There is plenty to do in the winery in the spring. The wines fermented and blended over winter are now ready for bottling. Still wines are bottled and sealed with a cork but, at this stage, the sparkling wines still have a long way to go. Additional live yeast and grape extract sugar are introduced to make a second fermentation in individual bottles: this is the same method as is used for making Champagne. The second ferment is sealed within the bottle to make the wine fizzy. Legend has it that sparkling wine was stumbled upon by a Benedictine monk, Dom Pérignon, some 330 years ago. He found bottles of wine exploding in his monastic cellar and discovered two important things: the wine had become fizzy because it had fermented a second time in the bottle and, more importantly, this sparkling wine was quite delicious!

A non-exploding bottle was produced in England with a 'punt' in the base to reinforce the glass, and thus Champagne was launched in the world.

REASONS TO GATHER AND CELEBRATE

Vineyard hospitality starts up in the springtime. Visitors come from all parts of the world for guided tours, picnics and of course to taste and buy our wines. Birthdays, marriages and celebrations throughout the year provide good excuses for families and friends to gather and party.

Easter is perhaps our favourite time for family celebrations here at Nutbourne. It is a bit like Christmas but without the excesses and all that present buying, plus we can usually expect some finer weather to be outdoors. There will be an egg hunt for the grandchildren (or several egg hunts by popular demand). There will be young calves nestled with their mothers in the field by the house and newborn lambs bleating in the lambing shed. And of course, there will be feasting (what did I just say about the excesses of Christmas?) – delicious cured salmon, wood pigeon, rabbit, new season salads and Bridget's amazing Simnel cake.

Another good excuse for a celebration is Mother's Day – mid Lent and three weeks before Easter. This shouldn't be a duty or a marketing opportunity for pubs and restaurants: it is a genuine chance to get family together at home and cook something delicious.

In Britain, for some reason, two of our eight Bank Holidays each year are in May. Perhaps it is because the English asparagus, new season lamb and early Kentish strawberries are so good we just need extra time off to indulge.

COOKING IN THE SPRING

We present a new season of culinary delights. Foraging in the countryside reveals
a treasure trove of new growth: wood sorrel, three-cornered leeks, wild garlic and
much more. Fresh new flavours enliven our cooking. The veg patch has a rainbow of
new salads and young vegetables on offer: baby beets, radishes, spring onions and,
later on, asparagus, purple cauliflowers, fennel and rhubarb. There is an abundance
of seafood from the wonderful British coastline – mackerel, crabs, scallops and wild
bass to name but a few. Our meat-eating repertoire can also be expanded using
wood pigeon, hare and rabbit.

Spring brings a yearning to eat lighter dishes with more colour and flavour than
calories. (Half my family are foolish enough to start a diet and jogging regime in the
early spring in order to be thinner and fitter for the summer ahead – I won't comment
on whether I see this working.) We all want food that reflects this exciting time of year.
I can particularly recommend Oliver's Chargrilled Cuttlefish recipe, with lovely tender
flesh, big flavours and stunning presentation, or our March Salad, with vibrant colours
of baby beets with tangy goat's cheese and wild garlic, or the Sea Bream Tartare, full
of freshness and taste.

We can also enjoy some springtime desserts: the indulgence of St George's Custard
Tart; home-grown rhubarb served in many guises; tangy Lemon Verbena Boodle; or
Bridget's rich, hugely satisfying Almond Polenta Cake. Those descriptions sound like
a fine wine – talking of which, Richard and I are delighted to introduce some amazing
wines. New Zealand Sauvignon is a perfect pairing for Crab Linguini, the Chianti is
delicious with the Wood Pigeon with Pickled Walnuts and our own field blend,
Nutbourne Sussex Reserve, is always very special. We describe this wine as 'the taste
of Nutbourne' – although it has been served for great occasions at Windsor Castle,
Buckingham Palace and many other famous places, there is nowhere it tastes better
than strolling through the vines where it originates.

THE COLOURS OF SPRINGTIME

Every season has its own palette. The spring landscape is about fresh greens, yellows and pinks under clear skies. The colours of nature are the natural partners for seasonal cooking. Asparagus is perfect with a sunshine egg yolk, pink lamb with scarlet rose petals or purple cauliflower with green samphire.

We have chosen one of Bridget's paintings to complement the food and wine in each month of the cooking year. This landscape of the Seven Sisters cliffs on the Sussex coast is matched to the calm delicacy of our Pinot Gris white wine. At first glance the painting is simple – the cliffs are chalky white, the fields green and the sky blue, but look more closely and you see a kaleidoscope of colour reflecting the complexity of both the subject and the wine.

March

New life, fresh green colours, the culinary aroma of wild garlic wafting down a country lane. Tender new leeks and baby beets, succulent fresh scallops, crab or wood pigeon and an abundance of delicate primroses to enhance every dish.

THIS MONTH'S FOOD CHAMPIONS	SOURCE	CHARACTER & COMMENT	RECIPES
wild garlic	shady banks in the countryside	fresh, aromatic, onion flavour	Wild Garlic Pesto, Crab Linguini, Wood Pigeon
beetroots	farm shops and other stores, or grow your own	sweet, rich and earthy	March Salad, Scallop Carpaccio
lemon verbena	garden centres for plants, specialist food stores for leaves	refreshing, fragrant, herby lemon	Scallop Carpaccio
leeks	all good greengrocers	mild, herbaceous, oniony	Haddock and Leek Gougère
Selsey crab	fishmongers (new season)	sweet, white meat and rich, wholesome brown meat	Crab Linguini
primroses	picked in the countryside	gentle floral flavour	Shed Chorizo, Rhubarb Crumble
wood pigeon	rough shooting, specialist food stores	very tender, mild, gamey	Wood Pigeon
rhubarb	all good greengrocers, or grow your own	tart, tangy, very fruity (it is, in fact, a vegetable)	Rhubarb Crumble

MARCH SALAD: BEETROOT, GOAT'S MILK CURDS & WILD GARLIC PESTO SALAD

SERVES 6

300g small, red beetroots

300g small, candy beetroots

1 tbsp white wine vinegar

150g goat's curd, or 100g soft goat's cheese and 50g plain yoghurt

3 tbsp Wild Garlic Pesto (see page 26)

salt and freshly ground black pepper

2 tsp pine nuts, toasted

Each month we present a champion salad to celebrate the things growing on our doorstep. Our March salad features red and candy beetroots complemented with goat's curd (a lovely light, tangy, soft lactic substance halfway to a goat's cheese) and our Wild Garlic Pesto (see page 26). I would always encourage chefs to be flexible – work with the ingredients you have or things growing in abundance rather than trolling the shops for an ingredient that proves difficult to source. With that in mind, goat's curd may be tricky to buy locally. If it's a problem, blending soft goat's cheese with plain yoghurt will make a good substitute.

1 Put the beetroots into a large saucepan, cover with cold water and add salt and vinegar. Bring to the boil over a moderate heat and cook the beets for 30 minutes. Drain and refresh under cold water.

2 Rub the beets with your fingers to remove the skin. Cut into wedges and arrange on individual plates.

3 Spoon dollops of the goat's curd on to the beetroot, then dot with the pesto. Finish with black pepper and a sprinkling of pine nuts.

**OLIVER'S TALES FROM A FORAGER'S DIARY
March – Wild Garlic**

Winter ends and spring begins when wild garlic appears from nowhere along steep banks and shady country lanes, growing in such abundance that no one can object to you gathering a few bundles. It is a forager's paradise! The young leaves are perfect in pasta dishes, salads or with pan-fried fish. We also make a pesto condiment that can be used in dozens of different dishes, and as a salsa or a marinade for barbecued meats. The season is short-lived but has a second phase when delicate white garlic flowers appear. These are a perfect addition to new season potatoes or grilled spring vegetables.

Many people prefer wild garlic to its cultivated cousin, the garlic bulb; it is somehow fresher and more fragrant. It is also free if you take the trouble to seek it out! I take a sack for gathering wild garlic leaves, and also a small basket for all the other delights that are starting to emerge in early March: wild chervil, lesser celandine, young nettles and primroses. There is nothing that lifts a plate of food more than a splash of colour from an edible wildflower.

SCALLOP CARPACCIO WITH BEETROOT PURÉE, CRÈME FRAICHE & LEMON VERBENA

There are some wines that cry out for a certain food accompaniment regardless of the season. Our very own Nutbourne Pinot Gris is one such wine – crisp, dry and citrussy with delicate spice. It inspired us to prepare a fish carpaccio where the unadulterated raw fish melts in your mouth in perfect harmony with the wine. You could use tuna, sea bass or salmon but we chose diver-caught king scallops from the western Scottish isles. The carpaccio is complemented with the sweetness of beetroot, the tang of crème fraiche, the freshness of lemon verbena and the smoky seasoning of burnt onion skin powder. Please don't be put off by the multiple elements involved in this stylish dish: the beetroot purée, lemon oil and onion powder are simple to prepare and extra delights worth having in stock to use on different dishes. These additions are also optional: the scallop will still be delicious without them.

SERVES 4 AS A STARTER

6 king scallops, shelled, rinsed and the hinge muscle removed

100ml crème fraiche

For the lemon verbena oil

20 lemon verbena leaves, finely chopped, plus extra to garnish

200ml rapeseed oil

For the beetroot purée

200g cooked baby beetroot

1 tsp malt vinegar

1 tbsp rapeseed oil

salt and freshly ground black pepper

For the burnt onion powder

skins of 3 brown onions

1 To prepare the lemon verbena oil, put the chopped verbena leaves in a jam jar, add the oil, close with a lid, shake well and leave for 24 hours to infuse. Use a sieve to remove the leaves when using the oil.

2 To prepare the beetroot purée, use a stick blender or food processor to blitz the baby beetroots, vinegar and oil to a smooth purée. Season the purée to taste and transfer it to the fridge to chill.

3 To prepare the burnt onion powder, preheat the oven to 190°C. Lay the onion skins on a baking tray and put in the oven for about 20 minutes until they are completely blackened. Transfer to a blender and blitz to a fine powder. Store in an airtight container.

4 To assemble the dish, slice the raw scallops into wafer-thin discs and arrange them on individual plates. Pipe on dots of the beetroot purée and small dollops of crème fraiche. Drizzle with lemon oil, sprinkle with onion powder and decorate with verbena leaves.

SMOKED HADDOCK & NEW SEASON LEEK GOUGÈRE

SERVES 6

For the choux pastry

50g unsalted butter

150ml water

70g plain flour

2 eggs

80g hard cheese, grated

salt and cayenne pepper

For the haddock filling

500g smoked haddock, boned

200g leeks, washed and finely sliced into rings

300ml milk

bay leaf

peppercorns

50g butter

50g plain flour

100ml white wine

1 lemon, zest and juice

2 fresh tarragon sprigs, stems removed, chopped

2 parsley sprigs, chopped

freshly ground pepper

fresh chives, snipped

leaf salad, to serve

I have included something with choux pastry in all my cookbooks and this is no exception: it is a very satisfying thing to make. Gougère is traditionally a cheesy choux ball, similar to a profiterole, but in this recipe, we are baking it in the shape of a nest with a delicious, rich, smoky fish filling. The result is a sort of fish pie but with the buttery flavour and crispness of a Yorkshire pudding.

1 Preheat the oven to 180°C. Begin by preparing the choux pastry. Put the butter with the water into a heavy-based pan over a high heat.

2 Just as the liquid rises up to boil, take the pan off the heat, shoot in all the flour and beat vigorously with a wooden spoon until smooth.

3 Return the pan to the heat and continue to beat for a couple of minutes to cook the flour.

4 Whisk the eggs in a bowl with a pinch of salt, then add them to the mixture, cook for a further minute, stir in the grated cheese and season with salt and cayenne pepper.

5 Transfer the pastry to a piping bag, then pipe a generous nest round the edge of a deep 18cm ovenproof dish. Place the dish in the fridge whilst you make the filling.

6 Put the haddock and leeks together in an ovenproof casserole. Pour over the milk, add the bay leaf and peppercorns (but no salt), cover with foil or a lid, then bake in the preheated oven for 20 minutes. Increase the oven temperature to 200°C.

7 Drain the cooking liquor from the fish through a sieve into a jug and reserve.

8 Melt the butter in a heavy-based pan over a moderate heat, stir in the flour and cook for 1 minute to form a roux. Keep stirring whilst adding the reserved cooking liquor, white wine and lemon zest and juice, a little at a time, until you have a smooth, thick sauce. Taste and season with freshly ground pepper.

9 Gently flake the haddock into the sauce together with the leeks. Spoon the filling into the choux pastry nest. Bake in the oven for 30 minutes.

10 Serve the haddock gougère hot from the oven with a sprinkling of chives on top and a leaf salad alongside.

WILD GARLIC PESTO

MAKES 2 X 250ML JARS

60g hazelnuts

**a large bunch of
wild garlic leaves**
(approximately 150g)

1 tbsp honey

1 tbsp cider vinegar

**60g hard goat's cheese
or Parmesan,** finely grated

200ml rapeseed oil

**salt and freshly ground
black pepper**

TIP We find that a hard
goat's cheese makes the
pesto light and special, but
it is sometimes difficult to find.
Grated Parmesan will do
just as well.

The first signs of spring are here at last – a touch of warmth in the
sunshine and a family outing to gather wild garlic leaves on the banks
of a shady country lane.

1 Begin by lightly toasting the hazelnuts in a hot, dry pan over a
moderate heat. Shake the pan so the nuts don't burn.

2 Put the hazelnuts, wild garlic, honey and vinegar in a food processor
and blitz to a pulp.

3 Add the grated cheese to the food processor.

4 With the blade of the processor still running, slowly add the oil a little
at a time to form an emulsion. Season well with salt and pepper.

5 Transfer the pesto to sterilized, airtight jars and store in the fridge.

SELSEY CRAB & WILD GARLIC LINGUINI

Selsey Bill is only about 25 minutes south of the vineyard: a perfect place to walk the dogs on a blustery spring morning, do a bit of foraging along the seashore, looking for early samphire or sea kale, and a great excuse to buy the seafood that Selsey is famous for. I am not going to suggest you make your own pasta for this dish: the fresh commercial brands are now so good. This crab linguini is intended as a very simple but luxury supper dish. It only takes minutes to prepare but, washed down with a crisp white wine, it is perfect for an intimate 'telly night in'.

SERVES 2

2 tbsp rapeseed oil

1 good-sized onion, diced

2 tsp curry powder

100ml white wine

1 lemon, juice and zest

150ml light crème fraiche

salt and freshly ground black pepper

400g fresh linguini

200g dressed crab, brown and white meat

80g samphire or sea kale, rinsed in cold water

18 wild garlic flowers, torn into pieces

1 fresh chilli, cut into rings

1 Heat the oil in a shallow pan over a moderate heat. Fry off the onion until soft but not browned.

2 Stir in the curry powder, wine, lemon juice and zest and the crème fraiche. Continue to cook for 5 minutes, reducing the liquid. Taste and season with salt and pepper.

3 Add a splash of oil to a big pan of lightly salted boiling water. Cook the linguini as specified on the packet. Drain, rinse the pasta under the tap to prevent it sticking, then tip it back into the pan to keep warm.

4 Add the crab, garlic flowers and samphire to the sauce. Stir over a moderate heat for a few moments. Fork the pasta into individual bowls, serve the crab sauce on top and finish with chilli rings.

TIP The flowers of wild garlic are less pungent than the leaves and great for this dish.

WOOD PIGEON BREASTS WITH PICKLED WALNUTS

Wood pigeon is a wild bird that is not in short supply. They are the bane of farmers because they feast on newly sown seeds and there are an awful lot of them in our delightful wooded English countryside. We have permission to shoot them the year round. Wood pigeon is a lovely lean meat to eat in the springtime. This recipe could not be simpler: it only takes a few minutes to cook and looks really stylish on the plate – very 'cheffy', as Oliver would say. Of course, if you are a purist, you will harvest your own fresh walnuts the previous summer and over several weeks, prick them with a needle, brine them, sun-dry them and eventually pickle. The lazy answer, however, is simply to buy a jar.

SERVES 4

1 tbsp rapeseed oil

20g butter

120g pork lardons

2 pickled walnuts, sliced

8 wood pigeon breasts, boned

salt and freshly ground black pepper

100ml red wine

a little Wild Garlic Pesto (see page 26)

young marjoram leaves

1 Put the oil and butter together into a heavy-based pan over a moderate heat. The oil prevents the butter from burning.

2 Add the lardons and fry until crisp, lift them out on to kitchen paper with a slotted spoon and keep warm along with the walnuts.

3 Season the wood pigeon breasts, then fry them for 2–3 minutes on each side. Lift these out of the pan and keep warm.

4 Turn up the heat, stir the red wine into the pan, season again, then boil rapidly for 1 minute.

5 Slice each breast into 2 pieces and arrange 4 pieces on each plate. Add the sliced walnuts and lardons, spoon the pan juices over, drizzle with Wild Garlic Pesto (see page 26) and finish with marjoram.

SHED CHORIZO

SERVES 4–6 AS A STARTER

500g minced pork

20g sweet paprika

15g smoked paprika

½ tsp chilli flakes

2 garlic cloves, finely diced

10g salt

2 tsp fennel seeds, toasted

50ml red wine

1 tbsp tomato paste

crispbreads, fried kale and plain Greek-style yoghurt, to serve

TIP The 10g of salt in this recipe is a specific weight to cure the pork – 2% of the weight of the meat.

The Shed restaurant in Notting Hill was launched by Richard and Oliver in 2012 and has been a major hit ever since. It really is a shed: it has a wooden roof and walls, it leaks in heavy rain, it's full of character and a trendy VIP haunt. Whether you are the Prince of Wales or America's number one recording artist, no one gives you a second look. Oliver's special recipe for chorizo has been on the menu since the day we opened. It is for sharing, served with creamy plain yoghurt, fried kale and crispbreads.

1 Put all the ingredients together into a large bowl and mix well with a wooden spoon.

2 Transfer the mixture into a container, packing it down tightly, then cover with a lid and transfer to the fridge to cure for at least 24 hours.

3 Place a heavy-based pan over a gentle heat. Add the meat mix and dry-fry without adding oil. The meat will cook through in 6–8 minutes and should be loose and crumbly.

4 Serve warm with crispbreads, fried kale and plain Greek-style yoghurt.

RICHARD'S WINE SHARING AND PAIRING It's Harvest Time...

...in the southern hemisphere anyway.

During my gap year travels I was a cellar hand in a Marlborough winery, pressing and processing literally thousands of tons of Sauvignon Blanc. Other grape types are grown in the region, but the SB dominates: there is hectare upon hectare as far as the eye can see. Now some of us tire of Sauvignon – the 'crisp green apple' and 'in-your-face' high acidity – but there are versions that really do stand out. Quality is firmly related to quantity. Top producers remove a lot of initial shoots, green-harvest and discard the lesser grape bunches. A really good producer will ripen only about a third of the yield that a mass production operator will go for. This gives much greater depth, sophistication and finesse to the finished wines.

So for March, let's celebrate the harvest taking place on the other side of the world with good NZ Sauvignon Blanc, such as St Clair, Dog Point or the famous Cloudy Bay. Pair any of these with the Selsey Crab and Wild Garlic Linguini and you may think you have gone to heaven. I also love the Wood Pigeon with Pickled Walnuts: for me this cries out for Chianti or any Sangiovese Italian red. As for the Rhubarb Crumble, there are some lovely 3–5 Puttonyos Tokaji that aren't prohibitively expensive – rich and generous, with great lasting orchard fruit flavours.

RHUBARB & HAZELNUT CRUMBLE

We all know how to make a crumble; it is among the first recipes our mothers ever taught us. But why not make the effort to cook a really special one for Mothering Sunday? The English rhubarb season is now in full swing. Enhanced with fresh oranges, a little spice and the crunch of hazelnuts, this is a timeless dessert that can't fail to please.

SERVES 6

For the fruit filling

2 oranges

600g rhubarb, washed and cut into 3cm lengths

2 tbsp runny honey

For the crumble topping

120g plain flour

75g butter, at room temperature, cut into small cubes

50g demerara sugar

1 tsp ground mace

50g rolled oats

50g hazelnuts, chopped

To serve

cream

primrose petals

1 Preheat the oven to 200°C. Grate the zest from the oranges, then peel and carefully cut out the segments without any pith.

2 Put the rhubarb pieces into a mixing bowl, add the orange zest and segments, stir in the honey and leave to macerate for half an hour.

3 Meanwhile, prepare the crumble crust. Sift the flour into another mixing bowl, add the butter cubes and work the two together with your fingers to form rough breadcrumbs.

4 Add the sugar, ground mace, oats and hazelnuts and mix in the same way.

5 Stir the rhubarb mixture again (it will have made some juice), then transfer to an ovenproof baking dish.

6 Spread the crumble mixture on top, place the dish in the preheated oven and bake for 30–35 minutes. The crumble should be golden brown on top with the filling bubbling through.

7 Serve piping hot with cream and a sprinkling of primrose petals to make it extra special for Mum.

ALMOND POLENTA CAKE WITH ROSEMARY SYRUP

SERVES 8–10

225g unsalted butter, softened

225g caster sugar

3 eggs

400g ground almonds

1 lemon, zest and juice

60g polenta flour

½ tsp baking powder

a pinch of salt

a little butter and plain flour for the cake tin

For the rosemary syrup

110g caster sugar

2 tbsp water

2 lemons, zest and juice

3 rosemary sprigs, stems removed

We often talk about food and wine pairings and particularly how well a certain white wine might complement seafood or the recommendation of a big red for a specific meat dish. However, it is much rarer to say, 'this is the wine to serve with cake'. Or, better still, 'this is the cake to serve with Champagne or English sparkling wine'. For me, this delicious almond cake infused with lemon and rosemary is the perfect partner for a good fizz. I am not one of those English wine producers who denigrates the 330-year tradition of Champagne. On the contrary, I adore the stuff; I more or less went into the hospitality world at a young age so I would have access to drinking it! But lots of the English sparklers, including our own, are now the equal to Champagne: we are achieving fabulous retention of fruit and fine balance; the biscuity character of ageing; and elegant spice and vanilla from time in oak barrels. Try this pairing, you won't be disappointed.

1 Preheat the oven to 175°C. Cream the butter and sugar together in a tabletop mixer until pale and fluffy.

2 Beat in the eggs one at a time, then add the ground almonds.

3 Remove the bowl from the mixer and use a spatula to gently fold in the lemon, polenta, baking powder and salt.

4 Butter a 20cm springform cake tin and dust the sides with flour. Transfer the cake mix to the tin and spread it out evenly. Cook in the preheated oven for 40 minutes.

5 Prepare the syrup. Put the sugar and water, the lemon juice and zest and the rosemary leaves in a small pan over a gentle heat; simmer for 10 minutes.

6 Check the cake is cooked through: it should be brown on top and moist in the centre. Remove the cake from the tin and place on a wire cooling rack. While the cake is still warm, use a skewer to prick the top all over, then pour the hot syrup over, allowing it to soak in.

7 Allow the cake to cool. Store in an airtight container until ready to serve with a delicious glass of ice-cold sparkling wine.

April

Vine buds burst open to unfurl their lime-green shoots. Nettles, spring onions, dandelions and green herbs follow suit. St George's mushrooms appear from nowhere, just waiting for the forager's basket.

THIS MONTH'S FOOD CHAMPIONS	SOURCE	CHARACTER & COMMENT	RECIPES
salmon trout	all good fishmongers	firm flesh, rich, almost gamey, sweet	Gravadlax
tender-stemmed broccoli	farm shops and all good greengrocers, or grow your own	wholesome, nutty, crunchy, similar to asparagus	April Salad
dandelion	in the garden, park or countryside	peppery, bitter, grassy	April Salad, Spring Onion Risotto
spring onion	farm shops and all good greengrocers, or grow your own	crunchy, pungent, spicy	Spring Onion Risotto, April Salad
St George's mushrooms	forage in the countryside	pale, earthy, textured	Spring Onion Risotto on St George's Day
cuttlefish	all good fishmongers	tender, elastic, buttery, mild	Chargrilled Cuttlefish
dill	farm shops and all good greengrocers, or grow your own	mild aniseed, citrus	Gravadlax
three-cornered leek	forage in the countryside	bright, fresh, crisp and herby	Rabbit Saddle

SALMON TROUT GRAVADLAX

**TO CURE ONE
WHOLE FISH
SERVES 16–20**

2–3kg whole salmon trout

large bunch of dill

large bunch of tarragon

4 tbsp sea salt

4 tbsp caster sugar

3 tsp juniper berries, crushed

4 tbsp gin*

TIP Ask your fishmonger to prepare the fish for you: fillet the two sides off the bone and leave the skin on.

Our family has a long-standing tradition of curing a whole salmon or sea trout to serve at special family feasts and celebrations. Although a large fish is an extravagance, gravadlax goes a surprisingly long way. You need a few days of curing, but there is nothing technical in the process and, once complete, it is a lovely moment to open the package and reveal the complete transformation of the salmon trout into a firm cured delicacy. Sections of the fish can be packaged and frozen for future occasions.

1 Inspect the fish fillets to make sure all bones have been removed.

2 Lay a large, double sheet of aluminium foil on a flat surface. Place one of the fish fillets on to it, skinside down, then scatter some of the herbs along it.

3 Mix the salt, sugar and crushed juniper together. Spoon this mixture evenly on top of the herbs. Layer with the remaining herbs, then spoon the gin over.

4 Place the other side of the fish on top, skinside up, to form a big sandwich. Then wrap the whole fish tightly in the double layer of foil, followed by cling film.

5 Place the package on a tray, put another tray on top, then weights on top of that. (A couple of large baked bean cans will do if you don't have kitchen weights.)

6 Place the weighted fish in the fridge for 48 hours; leave undisturbed.

7 After this time, discard the wrapping and juices. The gravadlax can be stored in the fridge for up to five days or portioned into sections and frozen.

8 To carve, place a section of the fish on to a chopping board, skinside down. Slide a sharp paring knife between the flesh and the skin and slide it horizontally, parting the skin from the flesh. Then carve across the grain into delicate slices.

Serve as a starter, on biscuits for a canapé or on a large platter for a buffet.

*The alcohol is optional but does give a lovely bite to the finished cure.

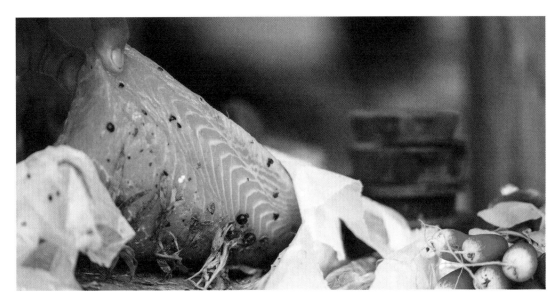

APRIL SALAD: TENDER-STEMMED BROCCOLI, DANDELION, RADISH, SPRING ONION, TOASTED HAZELNUTS & ASIAN DRESSING

It's not just about saving the planet: the best reason for eating locally grown vegetables in the prime of their season is that they simply taste so much better. No premature harvesting for the sake of appearance, no deep-chilled storage, no gassing in airtight packaging to extend shelf life – just real food plucked from the soil by hard-working hands. Tender-stemmed broccoli is a delicious vegetable to serve hot or cold. In this recipe it is blanched, then finished on a hot griddle and served warm. The young dandelion leaves give a subtle bite, the radishes and spring onions add freshness and the roasted hazelnuts complete the dish with a wholesome crunch. We have dressed this salad with a lovely Asian combination of soy, lime, chilli and syrup.

SERVES 6

400g tender-stemmed broccoli

80g hazelnuts

a good handful of dandelion leaves

6 radishes, sliced

4 spring onions, sliced

For the dressing

2 tbsp soy sauce

1 tbsp sesame oil

1 lime, zest and juice

1 tbsp golden syrup

1 fresh red chilli, finely sliced

1 Bring a large pan of lightly salted water to the boil. Add the broccoli and blanch for 4 minutes, drain, refresh under the cold tap, then put on to kitchen paper to dry.

2 Heat a ribbed griddle pan over a high heat. Toss the hazelnuts on to the griddle and roll them to quickly toast. (This really brings out the flavour of the nuts.) Remove the nuts from the heat and set aside.

3 Now put the broccoli on to the griddle, allowing it to char a little on all sides. Remove the pan from the heat.

4 Arrange a bed of dandelion leaves on a serving platter, put the broccoli on top and scatter with hazelnuts, radishes and spring onions.

5 Add all the ingredients for the dressing to a small pan and warm the mixture over a moderate heat. Use a whisk or stick blender to bring the dressing together, then pour over the salad and serve.

CHARGRILLED CUTTLEFISH, ROASTED PEPPERS, BLACK INK SAUCE

SERVES 4

600g cuttlefish, backbone removed

2 lemons, zest and juice

3 tbsp rapeseed oil

1 garlic clove, crushed

1 tsp fresh chilli, chopped

1 large red pepper

For the squid ink sauce

50g shallots, finely chopped

100ml fish stock

50ml dry vermouth

1 tbsp white wine vinegar

rock salt and freshly ground black pepper

1 tsp cuttlefish or squid ink

10g butter

This is such a visual and textural delight. The secret is minimizing the cooking of the cuttlefish: overcooking will make it tough and rubbery. I think this dish cries out for a sunny, crisp and herby white wine with a bit of body – maybe a Picpoul from southern France or a Grillo from Sicily. If we were in the vineyard we would drink our own Bacchus, a single varietal wine that has the fragrance and freshness to harmonize with the cuttlefish.

1 Using a sharp knife, score the cuttlefish flesh in a diamond pattern.

2 Place the cuttlefish in a bowl with the lemon zest and juice, the oil, garlic and chilli. Cover and leave to marinate in the fridge for at least 2 hours.

3 Cut the red pepper into pieces, discarding the core, then lightly brush with oil.

4 Place a ribbed griddle pan over a high heat and chargrill the pepper pieces until the skin starts to blacken. Remove from the heat and dice the flesh to make the pimento garnish.

5 To make the ink sauce, sweat the shallots in a lightly oiled, small, heavy-based pan over a moderate heat. When soft, add the stock, vermouth and vinegar, season, bring to the boil and reduce by half. Set aside, ready to finish the sauce when the cuttlefish is ready to serve.

6 Heat the ribbed griddle pan again over a high heat. When it is smoky hot, sear the cuttlefish together with the marinade juices for 1 minute on each side. The cuttlefish should colour on the outside but remain pearly within.

7 Reheat the sauce, whisk in the ink, then add the butter and whisk until thickened.

8 Carve the cuttlefish into generous chunks. Spoon the sauce on to the plate as a base, place the cuttlefish pieces on top and finish with diced pimento.

OLIVER'S TALES FROM A FORAGER'S DIARY
Prince William and the Royal Parks

I have been fortunate to cook for the royal family on many occasions; my father was regularly in charge of the kitchen for royal banquets at the most prestigious venues. But I have also had some more intimate times. When William and Kate were living at Kensington Palace they would come to our Shed restaurant, just round the corner, either for a 'date night' or with a few friends. Their security personnel would discreetly dine at another table and in that part of town no one took much notice.

I like to introduce the menu to special guests and explain where we source our ingredients. This went down well with the royal party. They were particularly enthusiastic to hear that the chickweed was plucked in Kensington Gardens. William said, 'You're doing such a good job reducing the weeds, please carry on.' I took this as royal approval to pick edibles in any royal park! A couple of weeks later, I was gathering magnolia petals in Hyde Park to make a springtime steep. I was approached by a park ranger who demanded to know what I was up to. I confidently told him I have permission from Prince William himself. The ranger just shrugged, got back on his four-wheeler and drove away.

I waved him off, saying, 'for King and country.'

ENGLISH CALF'S LIVER WITH PICKLED CUCUMBER, CRISPY BACON & RED CABBAGE

Why do we not eat liver more often? It is hugely nutritious, low in saturated fat and a real treat. There is somehow a belief that it is cruel to eat young calves but all right to drink milk and enjoy dairy products. For every cow born there is a bullock that is no use to the dairy but provides wonderful, grass-fed, rose veal. Like so many things we eat, the important thing to ask and to know is the provenance of the food we buy. We can then enjoy the delicious flavour and texture of calf's liver with a clear conscience. In this recipe we are enhancing the liver with sweet pickled cucumber, red cabbage and some crispy bacon.

SERVES 4

2 baby cucumbers

1 tbsp capers

small bunch of dill, chopped

2 tbsp cider vinegar

1 tsp sugar

salt and freshly ground black pepper

480g calf's liver, thinly sliced

2 tbsp plain flour

1 tbsp rapeseed oil

200g red cabbage, shredded

8 thin rashers of streaky bacon

1 Put the cucumbers through a spiralizer to make 'spaghetti' or, if you prefer, simply slice them thinly.

2 Mix the cucumber, capers, dill, vinegar and sugar together in a small bowl. Season well and leave for half an hour, to pickle.

3 Wash the liver under cold water, pat it dry with kitchen paper, then coat the slices in seasoned flour, ready for cooking.

4 Blanch the cabbage in a pan of lightly salted boiling water for 5 minutes, drain, return to the pan, sprinkle with rapeseed oil, season and keep warm.

5 At the same time, heat a ribbed griddle pan over a moderate to high heat. When it is smoky hot, cook the bacon rashers until crispy on both sides. Remove from the heat and keep warm.

6 Finally, cook the liver on the hot griddle for 1–2 minutes only on each side. The grease from the bacon should be sufficient to prevent it from sticking.

7 Spoon a ring of pickled cucumber alternating with red cabbage on to each plate. Add the liver straight from the griddle and finish with the crispy bacon.

SPRING ONION, BABY CARROT & MUSHROOM ORZO RISOTTO

SERVES 4

2 tbsp rapeseed oil

1 bunch of spring onions, sliced

1 bunch of baby carrots, sliced

1 fennel bulb, cored and diced

150g mushrooms, sliced

salt and freshly ground black pepper

300g orzo pasta

300ml vegetable stock

150ml white or rosé wine

1 bunch of dandelion leaves

1 tbsp poppy seeds

1 tbsp caraway seeds

There are so many delicious, tender young vegetables available in spring. For the forager, St George's mushrooms will appear on undisturbed grassy meadows and, for gardeners, dandelions will grow anywhere you don't want them! Markets and farm shops will also be full of new season mushrooms, spring onions, baby carrots and young leaves. This dish is a type of risotto but using orzo pasta instead of rice. The orzo is a lovely carrier of flavours and particularly good with a fragrant rosé wine alongside.

1 Heat the oil in a frying pan over a moderate heat. Add the spring onion, carrot and fennel and fry for 5 minutes, add the mushrooms, season well and cook for another 5 minutes.

2 Add the orzo to the pan and stir well to coat with oil. Pour in the vegetable stock and wine, a little at a time as it becomes absorbed, then continue to cook for another 5 minutes.

3 Check the seasoning, stir in the dandelion leaves and the poppy and caraway seeds. Serve right away.

ALBERT BRIDGE & BACCHUS WINE

Bridget's paintings are very diverse. We used to have a restaurant in Battersea that shared the same name as the vineyard: Nutbourne. Bridget was inspired to do a whole series of art in the immediate area. This lovely impression of Albert Bridge at night is used on our Bacchus wine label.

The vibrant quality and simplistic freshness of the image captures the essence of the wine. Sadly Nutbourne restaurant is no longer open. The property has been taken back by the landlord for redevelopment but, happily, the paintings live on.

STUFFED RABBIT SADDLE, THREE-CORNERED LEEK & PICKLED BEETROOT ONIONS

SERVES 4

1 rabbit, de-boned

6 three-cornered leeks, pulled from the ground and washed

150g lean pork mince

1 egg white

2 tbsp double cream

½ tsp ground nutmeg

salt and freshly ground black pepper

50g frozen pearl onions, defrosted and halved

1 pickled beetroot, chopped

50g smoked lardons

a dash of lemon vinegar

3 tbsp mayonnaise

wild chervil sprigs, to garnish

TIP Ask your butcher to skin and bone the rabbit. If you don't fancy eating rabbit – although it is quite delicious! – the recipe will work equally well with a boned chicken.

Rabbit meat is one of the forgotten joys of the English countryside. This dish is a perfect spring delicacy: boned saddle of rabbit stuffed with tasty three-cornered leeks and pork, served with bright red pickled onions and a tangy mayonnaise.

1 Preheat the oven to 160°C. Roughly chop 3 of the wild leeks. Put these into a food processor together with the pork mince, egg white, cream and nutmeg. Season well with salt and pepper, blitz until smooth, then transfer the mixture to a piping bag.

2 Place a long piece of cling film on the work surface and lay out the rabbit on top. Pipe a 2cm-wide strip of pork stuffing along the two loins. Now roll up the rabbit with the stuffing inside.

3 Wrap the cling film around the rabbit to form it into an even sausage shape, grip both ends of the cling film and roll the rabbit sausage along the work surface, screwing the ends tightly and squeezing out any air pockets.

4 Place the cling-filmed meat in a deep roasting tin, cover with water and season with salt and pepper. Put the tin on the hob and bring the liquid up to a simmer. Transfer to the preheated oven and leave to poach for 40 minutes.

5 Remove the rabbit from the oven, snip a small hole in one end of the cling film, drain out any liquid, then chill in the fridge.

6 Prepare the other elements of the dish. In a small pan, bring the pearl onions, beetroot and a dash of water up to boiling point, remove the pan from the heat and allow the onions to cool in the liquid.

7 Fry some lardons in a dry pan until crispy, then remove from the pan. Lightly cook the remaining leeks in the same pan. Set aside on kitchen paper.

8 Season the mayonnaise with lemon vinegar and black pepper, then transfer to a piping bag with a small nozzle, ready to finish the dish.

9 The rabbit saddle can be served hot or cold. To serve hot, remove the cling film, place the meat in a roasting tin with some butter and put in an oven, preheated to 200°C, for 10 minutes.

10 To serve, pipe a ring of mayonnaise around each plate and decorate with pieces of three-cornered leek, pickled onions, lardons and chervil. Carve the rabbit into even slices and arrange in the centre.

RICHARD'S WINES TO SHARE AND PAIR
The Lunar Calendar

You may think that the job of a restaurateur is about food and wine, but actually it is all about people. I spend my life talking – to customers, suppliers, staff, the media or just friends.

A worthy customer recently told me that to enjoy wine at its best we should use the biodynamic lunar calendar. Apparently, the moon's phases divide into fruit days, when most wine will taste at its very best; flower days, when aromatic and floral wines will show well; leaf days, when wine is not recommended but I am sure you can get away with the odd glass; and finally root days, when we should not drink at all. If I were a cynic, I would say this was a ruse to regulate wine consumption, but there is definitely some merit in the idea and it is fun to study the app.

All that being said, the highlight recipes for me this month are the Gravadlax – just sensational with very dry blanc de blancs sparkling – and the Stuffed Rabbit Saddle, which I would pair with a fine Beaune or Pommard red Burgundy – but only on a fruit day, of course.

ST GEORGE'S CUSTARD TART

Saint George is the patron saint of England, and he is celebrated each year on 23rd April, St George's Day. This is a day when we should all feast on new season asparagus, roast beef with St George's mushrooms (the first of the wild mushrooms found growing in little white rings on open grassland) and, for pudding, this lovely traditional custard tart. All very English and worthy of the saint who slew a dragon.

SERVES 8–10
FOR 25CM LOOSE-BOTTOMED TART TIN

For the pastry case

200g plain flour, plus extra for dusting

50g sugar

pinch of salt

100g butter, diced, plus extra for greasing

2 egg yolks

For the filling

400ml double cream

1 vanilla pod, split, seeds scraped out

8 egg yolks

100g golden caster sugar

ground cinnamon

1 Mix the flour, sugar and salt together in a large bowl. Use your fingertips to rub the diced butter into the mixture to form breadcrumbs.

2 Mix the egg with 1 tbsp water and pour into a well in the flour. Knead the dough together but don't overwork it.

3 Form the pastry into a ball, wrap it in cling film and chill in the fridge for at least an hour.

4 Preheat the oven to 200°C. Grease a 25cm loose-bottomed tart tin with a little butter. Sprinkle some flour on to the work surface and roll out the pastry to an even circle, a bit bigger than the tin.

5 Fit the pastry into the tin and neatly pleat around the edge with your finger and thumb; squeeze off any excess pastry.

6 Prick the base of the pastry case with a fork. Crumple a piece of baking paper, fit it inside the pastry case and fill with baking beans or uncooked rice.

7 Bake the case blind in the preheated oven for 10 minutes, remove the baking beans and paper, then bake again for a further 10 minutes. Remove the tin from the oven and reduce the oven temperature to 160°C.

8 Now prepare the custard filling. Put the cream, scraped vanilla and the pod itself into a heavy-based saucepan over a moderate heat and bring to the boil.

9 Beat the egg yolks and sugar together in a bowl until they become thick and pale. Pour the hot cream into the egg mix and whisk gently until combined.

10 Pour the mixture through a sieve into a jug, then carefully pour it into the pastry case, right up to the brim.

11 Place the tart in the oven and bake for 30 minutes, until the custard filling is just set.

12 Remove from the oven and allow to cool slightly. Before serving, dust the top with cinnamon then slice with a hot knife. Serve warm.

EASTER SIMNEL CAKE

SERVES 12

450g marzipan

icing sugar, for dusting

225g butter, softened

225g soft brown sugar

4 large eggs

225g self-raising flour

2 tsp ground cinnamon

225g sultanas

100g currants

100g glacé cherries, chopped

50g candied peel, chopped

grated zest of two lemons

4 tbsp rindless orange marmalade

beaten egg, to glaze

small chocolate Easter eggs and brightly coloured ribbons, to decorate

There are some things in a family that are simply expected. My grandmother used to bake a Simnel cake for Easter, complete with 11 marzipan balls on top to signify 11 of the 12 Apostles (Judas is left out for obvious reasons). Then my mother would always prepare a cake in the same way to serve on Easter Sunday. The mantle has since been passed to Bridget, who does her duty beautifully, and we hope our family will continue the tradition. In this recipe, we use plenty of cinnamon spice to enhance the dried fruits and layers of marmalade to add a nice tang, offsetting the sweetness of the marzipan.

1 Preheat the oven to 150°C. Oil the sides of a deep round 20cm cake tin and line the base and sides with baking paper.

2 Divide the marzipan into three equal amounts. Dust your work surface with a little icing sugar. Form two portions of the marzipan into rounds and roll these out to make two 20cm discs. Divide the remaining marzipan into 11 pieces and roll them between the palms of your hands to make them into small balls.

3 Put the butter, sugar, eggs, flour and cinnamon into a large mixing bowl. Beat together with an electric mixer, then stir in the dried fruits and lemon zest.

4 Put half the mixture into the cake tin in an even layer, then place a disc of marzipan on top.

5 Melt 2 tbsp of the marmalade in a small pan, then use a pastry brush to paint it on to the marzipan. Now add the second half of the cake mixture and smooth it out flat.

6 Bake the cake in the oven for 2½ hours. It should be risen, firm and golden.

7 Remove the cake from the tin, peel off the paper and allow it to cool on a rack.

8 Melt the remaining marmalade and spread it across the top of the cake. Place the second layer of marzipan on top and firmly press it down.

9 Brush the marzipan with beaten egg, then stick the 11 marzipan balls around the edge. Brush these with egg too, then either place the cake under a hot grill or scorch it with a blowtorch to brown the marzipan.

10 Before serving, decorate the cake with chocolate Easter eggs and bright ribbons.

May

English asparagus – pungent, irresistible and abundant. A rainbow of crisp and crunchy spring vegetables, the fragrant scent of chives, lovage and lemon verbena bring the natural flavours of the season.

THIS MONTH'S FOOD CHAMPIONS	SOURCE	CHARACTER & COMMENT	RECIPES
asparagus	farms, stores, markets – just make sure it's English	Marmite – love it or hate it. Tender, sweet, buttery and herbaceous	Roasted Asparagus, May Salad
radishes	gardens, markets, farm shops	crunchy, fresh, peppery	Carrot Hummous, May Salad
purple cauliflower	farm shops and all specialist greengrocers and growers	textured, nutty, wholesome and vibrant	Baked Sea Bass, May Salad
lemon verbena	garden centres, good greengrocers, or grow your own	intense, citrussy	Lemon Verbena Boodle
wild fennel	forage from dry ground, cliff tops, roadsides	herby, floral, aniseed	May Salad
sea bream	Cornish, line-caught blackhead or gilthead	succulent, meaty, mild flavoured	Sea Bream Tartare
rose petals	gardens or florists	sweet, spicy, aromatic	Lamb Rump
lovage	forage, garden or good greengrocers	celery without the texture; parsley with more bite	Buttermilk Quail
chive flowers	grow your own in a flowerpot	oniony, fragrant, visual	Roasted Asparagus, Buttermilk Quail

ROASTED ASPARAGUS, POACHED EGG & SAVOURY GRANOLA

SERVES 4 AS A STARTER

5 eggs

a dash of vinegar, for poaching

24 asparagus stalks

a drizzle of rapeseed oil

sea salt and freshly ground black pepper

For the granola

3 tbsp rolled oats

1 tbsp sunflower seeds

1 tbsp pumpkin seeds

1 tbsp hazelnuts, chopped

1 tbsp honey

1 tbsp rapeseed oil, plus extra for greasing

1 tbsp dark soy sauce

rock salt

a pinch of dried chilli

To finish

rapeseed oil

wild chervil

chive flowers

TIP Cooking a perfect poached egg with a runny yolk is best done in advance: they can be kept in the fridge to reheat at the last minute. In the ingredients list you will see that there are 5 eggs – one spare, in case you break one.

It's that time of year: the English asparagus season has begun in earnest and this delectable treat should be served as often as possible for the brief season, traditionally 23rd April (St George's Day) until 21st June. This recipe is a favourite: warm asparagus topped with a runny poached egg and finished with a seedy, nutty granola crunch.

1 Begin by preparing the granola. Preheat the oven to 180°C. Place all the ingredients in a large bowl and mix together. Transfer to a lightly oiled baking sheet, place in the oven and roast for 15 minutes.

2 Allow to cool, then store in an airtight container until needed.

3 To poach the eggs, bring a pan of water to the boil over a moderate heat. Reduce the heat to a simmer, add a little vinegar and salt to the water.

4 Break the eggs carefully into individual small dishes. Swirl the simmering water with a spoon to make a whirlpool, tip a single egg into the centre and cook for 90 seconds, then carefully lift out the egg with a slotted spoon and put it on to kitchen paper. Repeat.

5 Now we are ready to cook the asparagus and finish the dish. Preheat the oven to 220°C. Cut off any woody stems from the asparagus spears. Place them on a roasting tin, drizzle with oil, then season with sea salt and black pepper.

6 Place the tin in the oven and roast the asparagus for 10 minutes.

7 While the asparagus is cooking, bring a pan of water to the boil. Lower the poached eggs into the water with a slotted spoon and reheat for 60 seconds.

8 Arrange the asparagus on individual plates, place a hot poached egg on top, sprinkle with granola, then finish with a drizzle of oil, chervil and chive flowers.

SEA BREAM TARTARE, TOMATO, CUCUMBER & WASABI

Sea bream is a lovely fish to serve in its raw state. It has a gentle flavour but good meaty flesh that works perfectly with a little kick of wasabi to stop it being bland. Of course, we like to recommend our own wines with our own cooking and the Nutbourne Blush – delicate, sherbetty and very fresh – would be a delicious pairing. Alternatively, I would go to the southern hemisphere – a fragrant Argentinian Torrontés.

SERVES 4

350g sea bream fillet

1 lime, zest and juice

sea salt

½ small fresh chilli

2 firm but ripe tomatoes

½ cucumber

2 spring onions

1 slice sourdough bread or 2 tbsp breadcrumbs

2 coriander sprigs, shredded

1 tbsp rapeseed oil

salt and pepper

2 tsp wasabi paste

1 tbsp plain yoghurt

1 Skin the bream fillets (or ask your fishmonger to do so). Finely dice the fish with a sharp knife. Put it in a bowl with the lime, salt and chilli. Leave to marinate in the fridge for about an hour.

2 Cut the tomato into small cubes, discarding the seeds. Cut the cucumber, spring onion and bread into similar-sized pieces. Mix these together in a bowl and gently stir in the coriander, oil and seasoning.

3 Use an 8cm cooking ring to build small towers on individual serving plates. To do this, place the ring in the middle of the plate, spoon in an even layer of the tomato mixture, then spoon the diced bream on top. Press down gently with your fingers, then carefully twist the ring and lift it off.

4 Mix the wasabi with the yoghurt. Fill a small piping bag with the mixture and pipe a few dots on to the top of each portion.

OLIVER'S TALES FROM A FORAGER'S DIARY
The Crayfish Trap

I loved to create adventures in the wild with my young sons, and nothing is better than some old-fashioned trapping. We were looking for crayfish and had discovered an undisturbed stream that might yield what we were after. I baited my trap with cat food (apparently a favourite of the invasive American crayfish). We checked the trap every other day for a fortnight but no bites, so maybe it was the wrong time of the year. We gave up.

Two months later, now in May, I laid the trap again. The very next morning I found a small crayfish inside but, not to disturb things, I lowered the trap straight back into the deep water, hoping more would join. We revisited the trap a couple of days later, hugely excited with the anticipation of the haul. The net was now very heavy, and as I pulled it up, a huge fish was flapping inside.

We'd caught a pike as long as my arm: the one crayfish I left in the trap had been the bait!

Pike is a beautiful fish and interesting for a chef to fillet as it has an extra row of bones running through the loins. Carefully poached with wild fennel, with a creamy velouté sauce, the fish we caught was very fresh, rivery and delicious. It was also free food. To benefit from nature, you sometimes need both patience and luck.

MAY SALAD: WILD FENNEL, PURPLE CAULIFLOWER, ASPARAGUS & QUAIL EGGS

SERVES 6

1 purple cauliflower, cored and cut into florets

6–10 asparagus stalks, cut into 4cm lengths

12 quail eggs

a large handful of wild fennel fronds

2 fennel bulbs, cored and sliced

1 bunch of radishes, trimmed and halved

For the simplest of dressings

50ml virgin rapeseed oil

juice of 1 lemon

1 tsp Dijon mustard

1 tsp runny honey

salt and freshly ground black pepper

Look at the array of spring colours in this month's salad. Wild fennel is a wonderful free food that grows in abundance in south-east England. It has delicious aniseed fronds in the spring; in summer it will blossom, providing bright yellow fennel pollen; and in autumn the flowers will become crunchy, spicy fennel seeds. Unlike cultivated fennel, the bulb is not edible, so we have to grow or buy this separately. We are also using purple cauliflower – it's not just a visual delight, but also adds a delicious sweet, nutty flavour and is reputedly a very healthy thing to eat. Asparagus should, of course, be incorporated into every meal in May; when you tire of eating it straight up, it is a lovely addition to a salad. And finally, radishes and quail eggs provide contrasting gems of colour to finish off the dish.

1 Bring a large pan of lightly salted water up to the boil, add the cauliflower florets and cook over a moderate heat for 5–6 minutes, then lift them out with a slotted spoon and cool under running water; set aside.

2 Next, cook the asparagus for 3–4 minutes in a similar way.

3 Increase the heat and cook the quail eggs in the rolling boiling water for exactly 90 seconds, lift them out and immediately plunge them into a bowl of iced water. Leave the eggs for 5 minutes, then carefully peel off the shells. Cut each egg in half.

4 Casually assemble the cauliflower, the asparagus and the fennel fronds and bulbs in a large salad bowl. Arrange the quail eggs and radishes on top.

5 Put all the ingredients for the 'simplest of dressings' in a jar, seasoning well with salt and black pepper, then screw on the lid and shake for a few seconds. Dress the salad and serve.

BAKED SEA BASS, PURPLE CAULIFLOWER, SAMPHIRE & COCKLES

It is the time of year to start thinking about cooking outdoors – and what could be nicer than a Cornish wild sea bass baked over a wood fire and served with purple cauliflower, together with cockles and samphire foraged from the seashore? Wash this dish down with a glass or two of full-bodied white wine such as a New World Chardonnay and your first outdoor meal of the season will be something never to forget.

SERVES 4

a 1.2–1.6kg wild sea bass*

1 bunch of samphire

1 bunch of tarragon, stalks removed

4 spring onions, cut lengthways into thin strands

400g cockles, washed under cold water

100g unsalted butter, diced

1 lemon, zest and juice

1 tbsp white wine vinegar

freshly ground black pepper

1 purple cauliflower, cored and cut into florets

*Ask your fishmonger to clean the bass but leave it whole to get maximum flavour from the head and bones.

1 Preheat the oven to 220°C. Place a double layer of aluminium foil in a baking tray, ready to wrap the fish into a big parcel. Lay the bass on the foil. Combine the samphire, tarragon and spring onion and use the mixture to fill the cavity of the fish. Spread the remaining vegetables around.

2 Sprinkle the cockles over, then add the butter, lemon zest and juice and vinegar. Season well with black pepper but don't add salt – the samphire and cockles should provide enough of their own seasoning.

3 Wrap the whole combination into a tightly sealed parcel, then place the tin in the oven for around 12 minutes. (We use an outdoor wood fire so our temperature is not really regulated – but you can smell when the fish is cooked.)

4 Meanwhile, blanch the cauliflower florets for 4 minutes in lightly salted boiling water over a moderate heat. Drain and refresh under the cold tap.

5 Add the cauliflower to the roasting tin for the last 5 minutes of cooking.

6 Remove the tin from the oven and carefully open the parcel – it will have created its own delicious seafood butter sauce.

7 Cut tranches from each side of the bass and serve with the green vegetables, the cockles and the cauliflower florets. Spoon over the juices from the tin.

LAMB RUMP WITH MERGUEZ & ROSE PETALS

SERVES 4

2 pieces of lamb rump, each 200–250g

4 merguez sausages

2 pieces of crepinette, about 100g total weight

For the salsa

2 red roses (other colours can be used)

small bunch of flat-leaf parsley

1 lemon, zest and juice

1 tsp soft brown sugar

3 tbsp rapeseed oil

salt and freshly ground black pepper

Crepinette, also called caul fat, is a very thin, fatty membrane, usually lamb or pork, sold by specialist butchers. It is used to wrap around terrines, faggots, special meats or even fish to hold, protect, moisten and intensify flavour. The fat almost disappears during cooking. You can order it online. I would not normally suggest a recipe that uses a crepinette wrap. I have a delightful PA who has assisted me at the vineyard for many years and my test is always to ask, 'Jo, do you know what such and such is?' and then, 'Would you attempt this recipe for your family?' However, this creation of Oliver's was so delicious we decided we should give it a go. The effect of the crepinette is to infuse succulent lamb with the spicy flavours of merguez sausage; we then contrast this with an aromatic, floral rose petal salsa.

1 Preheat the oven to 210°C. Trim off the fat from the lamb rumps. Cut the sausage skins and squeeze out the meat.

2 Lay out the pieces of crepinette on the work surface, place a piece of lamb on each, then evenly spread the merguez meat on top.

3 Wrap the crepinette around to seal all sides. It does not matter if you have overlapping layers.

4 Prepare the salsa. Pluck off the rose petals, saving some to decorate the finished dish, and shred them into strips. Shred the flat-leaf parsley to match. Gently mix both with the lemon zest and juice, the sugar and the oil. Season to taste with salt and pepper; reserve at room temperature.

5 Roast the wrapped lamb in the oven for 15–20 minutes, depending how pink you like your meat.

6 To serve, slice each rump in half. Place one half on each of four serving plates and spoon a generous amount of the rose petal salsa on top, then scatter with the reserved rose petals.

RICHARD'S WINES
TO SHARE AND PAIR
The Bats are Back

A cool evening walk through the vines, with low orange light shining on to the lime-green shoots; the bats are beginning to dart low over the trellis, finding insects for supper. The effect is almost psychedelic.

This experience takes me straight back to my childhood here at Nutbourne. The farm seemed so huge and exciting then, with space for my brothers and me to hide, explore and find adventures. I remember being fascinated by the bats at dusk when I was only seven or eight years old. They then disappeared for many years, but now they are back.

The month of May gives the challenge of what wine to pair with asparagus. Even experts struggle with this, but for me it is aromatic whites every time – you need enough acidity and freshness to cut through the pungent aroma but also enough fruit and body to balance the fibre and buttery asparagus flavour. Dry German Rieslings, Alsace Sylvaner, Portuguese Alvarinho or English Bacchus all tick the box.

BUTTERMILK QUAIL WITH PEAS & LOVAGE

SERVES 4

4 quail

400ml buttermilk

1 tsp cayenne pepper

1 tsp English mustard powder

1 tsp salt

200g plain flour

1 tbsp onion powder

1 tbsp smoked paprika

salt and freshly ground black pepper

400ml sunflower oil

500g frozen peas

a knob of butter

small bunch of lovage leaves, shredded

chive flowers

TIP This recipe uses only the quail breasts. I would always make a stock with the remainder of the birds – but that is up to you.

This is a delicious, upmarket take on traditional Southern fried chicken. Quail has delicate, lean flesh, which thrives in the buttermilk marinade and lovage-flavoured peas.

1 Cut the breasts off each quail. Cut each breast in half and place them in a bowl with the buttermilk, cayenne, mustard powder and salt. Place in the fridge to marinate for a minimum of 6 hours.

2 In a shallow dish mix the flour, onion powder and paprika together and season well with salt and pepper. Lift the quail pieces out of the marinade, place in the seasoned flour; coat well on all sides.

3 Heat the oil in a heavy-based pan over a moderate heat. Fry the quail for a couple of minutes on each side. Transfer the meat to a roasting tin, ready to finish cooking in the oven.

4 Blanch the peas in lightly-salted boiling water for 2 minutes. Drain, add a knob of butter, then stir in the shredded lovage. Keep warm.

5 When you are ready to serve, put the quail pieces into a preheated oven at 180°C, for 8–10 minutes. Transfer to individual serving dishes, spoon over the pea mixture and finish with chive flowers.

CARROT AND CARAWAY HOUMOUS

Houmous is one of those lovely simple dishes that is greater than the sum of its humble vegetable parts. It is an ancient Middle Eastern emulsion traditionally made from chickpeas, tahini and olive oil – but these can be substituted with many alternatives. Peas or broad beans can be combined with mint if you are in the mood for green; use beetroot if purple is your thing; or sweet pepper and chilli if you are feeling fiery. We have gone for home-grown carrots with peanut butter in place of the tahini for a perfect orange 'sunshine' dip.

SERVES 6

For the houmous

600g carrots, peeled and cut into chunks

2 large garlic cloves, crushed

2 tsp caraway seeds

2 lemons, zest and juice

40g smooth peanut butter

rock salt and freshly ground black pepper

80ml rapeseed oil

To serve

2 heads of chicory, divided into leaves

1 bunch of radishes, washed, topped and tailed

1 Preheat the oven to 180°C. Place the carrots in an ovenproof dish and add the garlic, caraway and a little of the oil. Cook in the preheated oven (or in an air fryer) for 20 minutes, until the carrots are soft and a little singed.

2 Transfer the cooked mixture to a food processor, add the lemon juice and zest and the peanut butter, then season well with salt and pepper.

3 Blitz the mixture until smooth then, with the blade still running, slowly pour in the oil.

4 Transfer the houmous to a serving dish. Serve with chicory and radishes or other dippy things of your choice.

LEMON VERBENA BOODLE WITH THYME SHORTBREAD

Boodle is a cross between a syllabub and a trifle, named after the famous London club where Winston Churchill was a member. Our version uses tangy verbena leaves and the first blooms of elderflower. Served with thyme shortbread, it is a lovely pudding, perhaps with a refreshing glass of chilled pink fizz alongside.

1 Put the sugar and water in a small pan over a moderate heat, bring to the boil, then simmer until reduced by half. Take the pan off the heat and stir in the verbena leaves and elderflower. Leave to steep and cool for an hour.

2 Pass the syrup through a sieve and discard the leaves and flower heads.

3 Break the sponge fingers into pieces and use these to line the base of a serving dish.

4 Whip the double cream until it starts to hold its shape, then continue to whip while dribbling in the syrup until it is all incorporated.

5 Spoon the cream mixture over the sponge biscuits, transfer to the fridge and chill for an hour or more.

6 Now make the shortbread. Strip the thyme leaves from the stems, chop finely. You will need about 2 tbsp of chopped thyme.

7 Combine the flour, semolina, sugar, butter and chopped thyme in a mixing bowl. Work it together with your fingers to make a dough.

8 Sprinkle a little flour on the work surface and roll out the dough to less than 1cm thick. Cut into fingers, then place them on a baking tray lined with baking paper. Rework the offcuts of dough to use every morsel.

9 Chill the shortbread in the fridge for 30 minutes before baking.

10 Preheat the oven to 180°C. Bake the shortbread for 15–20 minutes until lightly golden. Remove from the oven and place on a rack, to cool.

11 Decorate the boodle with borage flowers. Sprinkle the shortbread with icing sugar and serve alongside.

For the boodle
SERVES 6
80g caster sugar
80ml water
6 lemon verbena leaves
4 elderflower heads
8 sponge fingers
400ml double cream
borage flowers, to decorate

For the shortbread
MAKES 12–16 BISCUITS
small bunch of lemon thyme
180g plain flour, plus extra for dusting
80g semolina
60g caster sugar
180g butter, softened
icing sugar

DARK CHOCOLATE & GRANOLA TIFFIN

MAKES 16 FINGERS

300g dark chocolate, broken into small pieces

150g golden syrup

2 tbsp cocoa powder

150g salted butter

150g granola

80g raisins

We include tiffin in every picnic at the vineyard and also offer it as a sweet finish on a Burger & Bubbly night: relaxed summer evenings with Gregory's Sussex Beef cooked on a vinewood barbecue. For me something rich, crunchy and chocolaty is the perfect foil for dry, smooth sparkling wine. This tiffin recipe uses dark chocolate to reduce the sweetness and granola instead of biscuits.

1 Put the chocolate, syrup, cocoa and butter into a dry bowl set over a saucepan of simmering hot water. Stir with a wooden spoon until the chocolate has fully melted and the ingredients are combined.

2 Remove the pan from the heat and stir in the granola and raisins.

3 Line a baking tray with cling film or baking paper. Spoon the mixture on to the tray and use a palette knife to firmly spread it into an even layer. Transfer to the fridge to set for 2 hours.

4 Turn the tiffin out on to a board, remove the lining paper and cut it into fingers or squares.

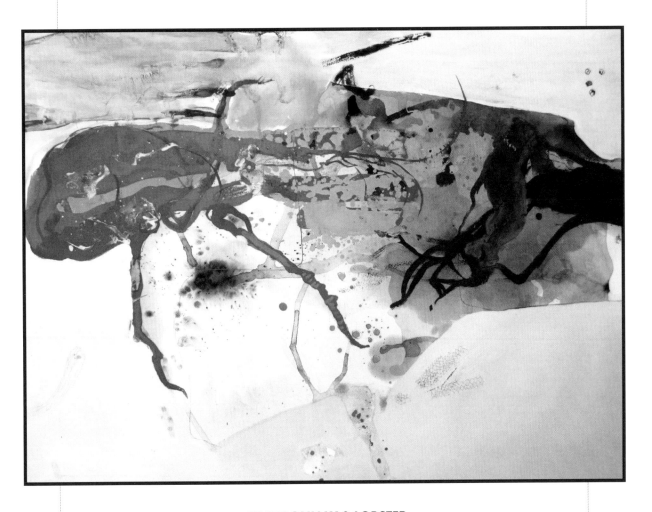

CHARDONNAY & LOBSTER

Bridget insists that she did not set out to paint a lobster but, when the creature 'appeared on the canvas', she simply enhanced it a little. This wonderful image has become synonymous with our single-varietal Chardonnay wine. It is the only wine we ferment from scratch in traditional oak barrels: the effect is a lovely, rounded buttery wine with lasting apricot, honey and a touch of gentle spice.

SUMMER

The days are long and warm, grandchildren
have the freedom to play in the garden and
we can eat and drink outdoors most days.
An English summer is a wonderful thing.
Of course, there are some days of rain, but our
gardens, parks and countryside are abundant
with foliage, flowers, smells and opportunities.
The long summer holidays give time for families
and friends to gather, celebrate, feast or just
chill together.

THE VINEYARD

The vineyard is now in full flight. Here at Nutbourne we have two marvellous Romanian ladies (mother and daughter) who nurture the vineyards throughout the year. We have 26 acres under vine and we estimate that between us each plant is individually handled seven times during the growing season. Small inflorescences appear in early June and flowering starts two or three weeks later. A vine self-pollinates so we want warm, dry days with a light breeze to successfully set the fruit. We continue to control the leaf canopy throughout July – thinning where there is too much growth, stripping off the leaves that shade the emerging bunches and sometimes green-harvesting to discard smaller grapes which won't fully ripen.

Gregory sows cover crops down the rows. He has developed a growing programme using mustard seed, which creates natural sulphur, and linseed, which is good nourishment for the vines. This is multi-purpose regenerative farming at its best. The cover crop provides natural minerals to help prevent disease and subdue the weeds, loosens the soil and, when eventually mowed in, delivers green compost around every plant.

We also have undisturbed areas of wild flowers, wetlands and wilderness surrounding the vineyard. This encourages insects as well as ladybirds and butterflies, which, while not required for pollination, feast on tiny pests that harbour in older vinewood. The insects also attract more small birds, which in turn attract larger birds of prey – these then become the protectors of our crops from pigeons and small mammals. Although a vineyard is an intensive cultivation of the land, with all these factors, I am pleased to say that well managed viticulture in the UK is proven to be climate positive – reducing carbon and building biodiversity.

THE WINERY

This is at its most inactive in the summer months, although there remains a constant requirement for labelling, packaging and dispatching of orders, plus the final process of making traditional-method sparkling wine. Producers in the Champagne region often claim that their wine is finished 'á la volée' (in flight), but I suspect this is rarely the case, at least not for all their production. As I explained in the introduction to Spring, our sparkling wines are made using a second fermentation in individual bottles. This is by far the best way to create sparkling wine, but does leave a sediment in the bottle. The Champenoise perfected a technique for dealing with this. The wine is matured horizontally, then carefully transferred to a 'riddler' where it is slowly turned and tilted until the bottle is vertically upside down with the sediment collected in the bottle neck. The bottle neck is then frozen and 'disgorged' – a process of removing the cap and allowing the pressure of the sparkle to shoot out the frozen sediment, leaving just pure, clean wine in the bottle. There are, of course, machines that do all these things automatically. At Nutbourne we admit to using an electric giro-pallet for the riddling process, but we still disgorge 'á la volée', using a small hand tool, one bottle at a time. Many a summer's afternoon is spent doing this. Olivia and I can process 500 bottles in a session. There must be a reward at the end of it – it's very important to check your own product. There's nothing like a freshly disgorged glass of crisp English sparkling, gentle bubbles rising with hints of the countryside in which it has been created.

VISITORS, FEASTING AND CELEBRATIONS

Whilst I have said that the summer is the down season for winemaking, this is more than compensated for with the constant flow of visitors to the vineyard. More people come each year to explore, taste and learn about the growing and production of English wine. Any excuse will do, a hen or stag outing (sometimes a challenge to get them to concentrate), wine clubs, corporate team outings, picnics, birthday parties (the more senior variety) or the odd small wedding (we are very picky and make sure it is really a rustic vineyard they are looking for).

We host pop-up dining evenings in the vines or wine lodge throughout the summer months. These involve the whole family and, although it is a commercial venture, I think we enjoy these evenings as much as our customers. We present multi-course extravaganzas using wonderful produce that we either grow, forage or source locally and combine it with an array of our own wines. We vary the location of the dining and give detailed explanations of the food and wine pairings, much to the amusement of the enthusiastic diners.

At the more casual end of the scale, Gregory and Lani take the lead for a different type of vineyard hospitality called Burger & Bubbly – but more about that in July, when we have included a recipe for making and cooking the ultimate beef burgers at home. Of course there are also excuses throughout the summer for outdoor parties at home. Isn't that why God invented Sundays?

THE COOKING AND FLAVOURS OF SUMMER

The basic rule is that anything we can cook on a barbecue should be. Combine this with making best use of the vegetable garden and the abundance of fruits for pudding and we are well on the road to a blissful culinary summer. I think each of the summer months has its own definitive scent: wafting elderflower or freshly picked strawberries in June; a hot earthy smell of newly-dug carrots in July enhanced with flowering marjoram and thyme; and then in August the overwhelming perfume of sun-ripening tomatoes with basil planted as a companion crop beneath. These aromas capture high summer even with your eyes closed.

Summer is an opportunity for your cooking to be plant-led – so we have included loads of salad and vegetable recipes. I am not suggesting giving up meat or fish altogether – that is up to you – but if we let the plants lead the menu, the proteins can fit in on the side. This tends to mean you serve smaller portions of meat or fish – a rebalance in your diet that can only be good for a few months of the year. Try the Pea & Mint Velvet with just a few morsels of smoked salmon, or field mushrooms with a little richness from blue cheese and the lovely tang of freshly picked redcurrants.

The barbecue is a hugely versatile cooker, it just takes practice. Oliver uses a wood-fired oven alongside his grill, both fuelled with old vinewood. Try chargrilled courgettes, red snapper or lamb's kidneys cooked in this way. Cold dishes too are great in the summer; they can be ready in advance and then taken on a picnic or just casually brought out of the fridge ready to eat. So many edible flowers are available from the vegetable garden and the wild that there is no excuse – every dish can be beautiful.

The range and choices for desserts must be based around the abundance of ripe summer fruits. Starting with strawberries, then currants, raspberries, loganberries and gooseberries. This moves into the stone fruit season: cherries, greengages, plums and even peaches are now grown commercially down in Kent. Try the Peach Melba recipe or Berroffee pie, a hugely indulgent summertime take on the classic Banoffee pie.

WHY CAN'T THE SUMMER GO ON FOREVER?

We subject our visitors to Bridget's art at every turn – not just on the wine labels, but her work is also displayed on the walls of the winery, both inside and out. It inspires other artists to visit and find a quiet spot in the vines to paint. There is natural art everywhere in the vineyard, changing colours at different times of day, shafts of sunlight picking out the shape and composition within the trellis. Try lying on your back under a vine, look up to the sky through the leaves and discover infinite patterns and designs. In the painting above, Bridget has captured the vineyard heat on canvas using steamy hot colours of pink, orange and green. We use this image on the label of our delightful dry, sherbetty Blush Rosé wine.

June

Tiny white flowers that are only just visible on the vines are pollinating in the breeze. The vegetable garden is brimming with new produce and culinary opportunities.

THIS MONTH'S FOOD CHAMPIONS	SOURCE	CHARACTER & COMMENT	RECIPES
elderflower	trees and bushes in the countryside and parks	a smell and flavour like no other: floral, sweet, summery	Elderflower Champagne, Scallops, Posset
kohlrabi	veg garden or good greengrocers	fleshy, peppery turnip radish	June Salad
courgettes	all greengrocers	rich and tender, a great carrier of other flavours	Chargrilled Courgettes
Alexander leaves	foraged in the wild	moreish, mildly bitter, crisp	Pea & Mint Velvet
garden peas and broad beans	veg garden, markets and stores – make sure they're British	the best are the freshest home-grown	Pea & Mint Velvet, June Salad, Scallops
marigolds	flowerpot, window box or garden	the ultimate vibrant edible petal	Chargrilled Courgettes
scallops	good fishmongers; make sure they're sustainable, 'diver-caught'	succulent, moreish	Scallops
lamb sweetbreads	specialist butchers	special, exotic, delectable	Lamb Sweetbreads
wild strawberries	foraged on banks, in woodlands and dry soil	delicate, tangy, exquisite	Posset
home-grown berries	veg garden, all good greengrocers	the taste of an English summer	Berroffee Pie

CHILLED PEA & MINT VELVET WITH SMOKED SALMON

SERVES 6 AS A STARTER

For the pea velvet

40g butter

½ small onion, finely diced

1 celery stalk, finely diced

1 carrot, peeled and finely diced

salt and freshly ground black pepper

40g plain flour

600ml chicken stock

400g frozen petits pois

fresh mint leaves, shredded

To finish

150g smoked salmon pieces, shredded

100ml crème fraiche

Alexander leaves, shredded

This was one of Bridget's moments of genius – a delightful, chilled, flavoursome summer soup with the surprise addition of smoked salmon turning it into a glamorous new starter. We are, however, presenting an English Vineyard Cookbook, so we don't want to call the soup the classic French term, 'velouté'; instead, we have simply called it 'velvet'.

---

1 Put the butter in a heavy-bottomed pan and melt over a gentle heat.

2 Toss in the 'mirepoix' of diced vegetables – onion, celery and carrot. (These can be what you have in the veg rack: we just want some flavour.) Season with salt and pepper.

3 Cook for 2 minutes but be careful not to brown the butter or the vegetables.

4 Increase the heat and stir in the flour to make a roux. Allow the flour to cook for a minute, then whisk in the stock. After another couple of minutes, add the peas.

5 When the peas have cooked, transfer the mixture to a food processor, add the mint leaves and blitz to a smooth purée. Check the seasoning,

6 It is nice to serve a cold soup in chilled bowls. When you are ready to serve, ladle the 'velvet' into individual dishes, place shredded smoked salmon in the centre, add a teaspoon of crème fraiche and finish with shredded Alexander leaves.

CHARGRILLED COURGETTES WITH GIANT COUSCOUS, RED ONION & MARIGOLD

If you grow courgettes, you will know that they provide such a bountiful crop, you have to find different ways to enjoy them throughout the summer. This simple chargrilled starter combines delicious flavours and textures: dukkah spices to season, giant couscous for nutty texture, plain yoghurt, red onion and black onion seeds to add bite, then marigold petals and parsley to finish.

SERVES 4 AS A STARTER

3 large courgettes

a drizzle of rapeseed oil

2 tsp dukkah spice mix

200g giant couscous

100ml Greek-style plain yoghurt

salt and pepper

1 small red onion

flat-leaf parsley

onion seeds

marigold petals

1 Cut the courgettes into even slices. Lay them out on a tray, drizzle with oil and sprinkle with dukkah spices.

2 Place a ribbed griddle plate over a high heat and allow it to get smoky hot. Sear the courgette slices for just a few seconds on each side. Set the courgettes aside and allow to cool.

3 Cook the couscous in lightly-salted boiling water for 6 minutes. Drain, rinse under the cold tap and allow to cool.

4 Prepare the other elements of the dish. Season the yoghurt with salt and pepper, slice the red onion and shred the parsley.

5 Arrange the courgette slices on individual plates. Scatter the couscous on top, spoon the yoghurt in the centre, then top with raw red onion, onion seeds, parsley and marigold petals.

ELDERFLOWER CHAMPAGNE

MAKES 5 LITRES

20 elderflower heads
(pink ones are wonderful
if you can find them)

4.5l water

1kg sugar

3 lemons, juice and peel,
pith removed

There is nothing quite like the heady aroma of elderflowers along the hedgerows – for me, it heralds the start of the English summer. A lot of elderflower Champagne recipes use wine yeast to produce a wine-style bottle fermentation with around 8% alcohol. This old-fashioned country recipe relies on the natural yeasts of the flower heads to create a ferment and should produce a gentle fizz with only around 3% alcohol – perfect for a lazy summer picnic.

1 Make sure the elderflower blossoms are clean and dry. Place half the water together with the sugar in a large pan over a moderate heat and bring to the boil. Make sure the sugar is completely dissolved.

2 Transfer to a clean, sterile bucket; add the remaining water, plus the lemon juice and peel.

3 Allow the mixture to cool to room temperature, then stir in the elderflower heads. Place a cloth over the top of the bucket and leave in a warm shady place.

4 Stir twice a day for 2 days: the ferment should start to bubble on the top.

5 After this time, pour the liquid through a sieve, then decant into traditional airtight glass-stoppered bottles. Leave in a cool place for 2 weeks. You can check the ferment from time to time by releasing the glass stopper. Please note: too much pressure could cause the bottle to explode.

6 Serve the Elderflower Champagne well chilled, with a garnish of fresh elderflower blossom.

**OLIVER'S TALES FROM
A FORAGER'S DIARY
Elderflower Explosion**

When we lived in London, the only tree in my garden was a pink elderflower. During the Covid lockdown we maintained contact with our restaurant customers with foraging recommendations, including a recipe and full kit for DIY elderflower Champagne.

All they had to do was venture out to pick the flowers to create a most delicious, refreshing, mildly alcoholic beverage.

I made a few trial batches using my pink elderflower heads, which gave it an irresistible blush colour. One night I woke with a jump. Hearing a bang and thinking there was someone in our understairs cupboard, I investigated, only to

find my Elderflower Champagne was in full ferment and a cork had fired off a bottle. I quickly pushed the remaining corks in as hard as they would go and transferred them to the fridge.

This was the most successful drink I have ever made – but remember, it is my brother who makes the real wines at the vineyard.

JUNE SALAD: KOHLRABI, GOAT'S CHEESE & BROAD BEANS

Our June Salad is a little different, using the lovely crunch of kohlrabi with shaved goat's cheese and broad beans. This is a garden dish to enjoy with a chilled glass of delicate rosé wine – Provençal, Anjou or Sussex – on one of the longest days of the year.

SERVES 6

1 large kohlrabi bulb

100g hard English goat's cheese

100g broad beans

40g almond nibs

rock salt and pink peppercorns

dill sprigs

virgin rapeseed oil

1 Peel the kohlrabi with a wide-mouthed peeler. Cut it into 4, then slice as thinly as possible, on a mandolin or with a very sharp knife. If you are not using the slices right away, put them in a bowl, cover with cold water and add a little lemon juice.

2 Remove the broad beans from their long pods and cook them in lightly-salted boiling water for 2 minutes. Drain, refresh and, as soon as they are cool enough to handle, squeeze out the kernels; discard the outer skins.

3 Shave the goat's cheese, again using a wide-mouthed peeler.

4 Assemble the salad in layers of sliced kohlrabi, cheese shavings and broad beans. Finish with a sprinkle of nibbed almonds, rock salt, pink peppercorns, dill sprigs and a drizzle of oil.

KING SCALLOPS, CRISPY BACON, PEA & ELDERFLOWER

SERVES 4

200g frozen peas

salt and freshly ground black pepper

a knob of butter

a dash of cream

4 thin rashers of streaky bacon

16 king scallops

100ml white wine

2 elderflower heads, individual flowers snipped off with scissors

a few pearl onions soaked in beetroot juice (see page 48)

Seared scallops are a truly luxurious thing to eat. They don't need too much competition from other flavours, so in this recipe we are just using the saltiness and crunch of crispy bacon, the wholesome body of peas and the unusual sweet, floral flavour of elderflower. We think of the elderflower season as a chance to make cordials, jellies and desserts, but actually the fragrant blooms are a wonderful enhancement for savoury dishes as well. Oliver was still living in London during the first Covid lockdown and the one thing his small garden boasted was a pink elder tree. With restaurants closed and compulsory home isolation, he developed this lovely dish, celebrating the season for these sweet, aromatic, early summer flowers.

1 Bring a small pan of lightly-salted water to the boil over a moderate heat. Add the peas and cook for 3 minutes, then drain and refresh under the cold tap.

2 Transfer half the peas to a small bowl. Add a knob of butter and a little cream, season with pepper, then blitz into a purée. Keep both the purée and the whole peas warm, ready to serve with the scallops.

3 While the peas are cooking, place a ribbed griddle pan over a moderate to high heat. Cook the bacon rashers in the pan until crispy, lift off on to kitchen paper, then snip into pieces, ready to serve.

4 Keep the pan on the heat with the fat from the bacon still in it. Season the scallops with salt and pepper, add to the pan and sear them for just 1 minute on each side. Add the wine and half the elderflowers to the hot pan – it will sizzle. Lift out the scallops and transfer to a warm plate. Meanwhile, let the juices bubble and quickly reduce by half.

5 Arrange the scallops and bacon on individual plates. Spoon a few dollops of the pea purée alongside, scatter with whole peas and decorate with pearl onions and the remaining elderflowers.

6 Serve the white wine reduction separately or spoon it over at the very last minute.

PORK SCHNITZEL, FENNEL, APRICOT & MARJORAM

Why do we think of a schnitzel as an old-fashioned dish? When Oliver produced them on a flaming hot day for a lunchtime gathering in the vineyard, there was a fair amount of derision, especially from his brothers. But when the feasting began, these succulent slices of tender pork topped with a crisp, sweet, herb salsa were something else. We served them with our much-loved Sussex Reserve – elderflower on the nose, soft fruit on the palate and lasting acidity. The secret of a good schnitzel is to coat only lightly in breadcrumbs, shallow fry in hot, clean cooking oil and serve right away.

SERVES 4

For the salsa

1 fennel bulb, finely diced

80g dried apricots, chopped

1 tbsp marjoram, chopped

1 tbsp rapeseed oil

1 tbsp lemon juice

salt and freshly ground black pepper

For the schnitzels

100ml sunflower oil

4 pork escalopes, each 100–120g in weight

2 tbsp plain flour, seasoned with salt and pepper

2 large eggs, whisked

100g breadcrumbs

To finish

flat-leaf parsley

mustard seed flowers (optional)

1 Begin by preparing the salsa. Mix all the ingredients together in a bowl, season well, taste and season again. Leave to develop for at least 1 hour.

2 Heat the cooking oil in a frying pan over a moderate to high heat. It is worth testing the temperature before cooking by floating a small piece of bread in the oil.

3 Use 3 separate flat plates for the flour, egg and breadcrumb so you can quickly coat the meat. Lightly place a slice of pork in the flour; next coat in egg, allowing any excess to drip off; then lightly coat in the breadcrumbs.

4 Shake off any excess crumbs, then immediately lay the escalope into the hot oil. Repeat with the other slices and cook each one for about 2 minutes on each side. Lift them out on to kitchen paper to absorb any excess oil.

5 Serve the schnitzels with the fennel and apricot salsa spooned over, garnished with a few parsley leaves and mustard flowers. I recommend a leafy green salad and a bowl of steamed new potatoes to go with it.

LAMB SWEETBREADS & CUTLETS WITH MORELS

SERVES 4

200g lamb sweetbreads

2 tbsp plain flour, seasoned with salt and pepper

4 morel mushrooms

100ml dry sherry

100ml water

1 small rack of lamb

100g butter

1 tsp fresh thyme, chopped

1 garlic clove, crushed

4 radishes, trimmed and sliced

80g peas, cooked

pennywort leaves

We associate lamb sweetbreads with Michelin-starred menus and something not to be attempted at home. However, they are available from specialist butchers and are a wonderful thing to eat alongside new-season lamb cutlets. You will also need to be a very experienced or lucky forager to find morel mushrooms in the UK. They sometimes appear under ash or conifer trees, but also on sandy golf courses! (Make sure that any golfing members of the family have a firm brief to be on the lookout.) Fortunately, dried morels are readily available: soaked overnight, they provide tremendous flavour to enhance this special dish. We could not resist photographing this dish alongside our own Pinot Noir red wine. What a fabulous pairing!

1 To prepare the sweetbreads, first soak them in salted water for one hour, rinse, then soak in fresh salted water for another hour. Rinse again, carefully trim off any fat, remove sinews, then cut into bite-sized chunks. Dry them on kitchen paper, roll in seasoned flour and set aside in the fridge, ready for cooking.

2 Mix the sherry and water together and season with salt and pepper. Add the morels and leave to soak for 2 hours. This liquid will provide a lovely base for the jus.

3 Preheat the oven to 190°C. To prepare the lamb rack, trim off alternate bones to leave 4 good-sized cutlets. Place the rack in a small roasting tin and cook in the oven for 12–15 minutes (or use an air fryer). When cooked, keep warm and allow to rest.

4 Heat the butter in a small heavy-based pan over a moderate heat. Fry the garlic and thyme for 1 minute, toss in the sweetbreads and fry gently on all sides for about 5 minutes.

5 Lift out the sweetbreads and keep them warm. Add the mushrooms and their juices to the hot pan and boil rapidly to reduce by half.

6 Carve the rack into 4 cutlets. Arrange these on individual serving plates together with the sweetbreads, radishes, a scattering of peas and pennywort leaves. Spoon the hot jus over and serve.

BERROFFEE PIE

This is our version of a classic banoffee pie using strawberries, raspberries and blueberries in place of bananas. The original recipe was created at The Hungry Monk restaurant in East Sussex in the early 1970s. We have retained the concept of boiling an unopened tin of condensed milk to make the most delicious caramel.

SERVES 8–10

400g can of condensed milk

225g Hobnobs or digestive biscuits

100g butter

pinch of rock salt

250ml double cream

2 tbsp elderflower cordial (optional)

150g strawberries, cut into quarters

100g raspberries

100g blueberries, cut into halves

50g hazelnuts, crushed and lightly toasted

1 Place the tin of condensed milk (unopened) in a small saucepan, cover with water, bring to the boil, then simmer over a low heat for 2 hours. Make sure you occasionally top up the water, if necessary.

2 Line a 20cm loose-bottomed tart tin with a disc of greaseproof paper. Crush the biscuits or blitz them in a food processor. Melt the butter, mix it into the biscuit crumbs, then press the mixture into the tin to make an even base. Chill in the fridge for an hour, until firm.

3 Allow the heated condensed milk to cool, then open the can – it will have transformed into a thick golden caramel. Stir in a pinch of rock salt, then spoon the caramel on to the pie base and spread in an even layer.

4 Whip the cream until firm, then fold in the elderflower cordial.

5 Spread a layer of the cream on top of the caramel, then decorate with strawberries, raspberries, blueberries and toasted nuts.

6 Slice, serve and enjoy! Add a dollop of ice cream on the side if you really want to go all out.

**RICHARD'S WINES TO SHARE AND PAIR
For the Love of Lunch**

The romance of a vineyard exists the world over and time spent there is always worthwhile. It is a place to walk and talk, a place to enjoy nature, or a place to fall in love.

Long, leisurely lunches are one of life's great pleasures and there is nothing quite like al fresco dining in the vines. It is more than location, fine wine, delicious food and good company: it is a whole sensory experience.

The Pea & Mint Velvet is a delight on a hot summer's day, perhaps with an Austrian Grüner Veltliner or an Italian Gavi di Gavi. I loved the sweetbreads recipe and would recommend a Pinot Noir from Oregon or Central Otago in New Zealand. And as for the Berroffee Pie, I do recommend something tart, fruity, fizzy and English. I will say no more!

WILD STRAWBERRY & ELDERFLOWER POSSET

SERVES 4

3 large elderflower heads, lightly rinsed

600ml double cream

160g caster sugar

3 lemons, zest and juice

60g wild strawberries (or cultivated strawberries if you are not a forager)

wild berries and edible flowers, to decorate

It is the season of elderflowers and strawberries and they make wonderful partners. Wild strawberries are hard to find, but it is like discovering hidden treasure when you do: tiny jewels nestling among dandelions and daisies along dry, shaded banks. But I will forgive you if you simply buy some locally-grown cultivated berries to make this recipe. This posset captures the deep tangy flavour of wild berries with the sweet bouquet of elderflower – a delightful combination.

1 Put the flower heads in a small pan, pour the cream over and place the pan on a low heat.

2 Bring the cream to scalding point (not quite boiling), remove the pan from the heat and leave to steep for 20 minutes.

3 Carefully strain out the flower heads from the cream, then return the pan to the low heat. Add the sugar and stir until dissolved, then add the lemon zest and juice. The mixture will thicken at this point.

4 Hull the strawberries and distribute them evenly between 4 shallow serving dishes. Pour the cream mixture over the berries, then transfer the possets to the fridge to set.

5 Decorate with some additional wild berries and edible flowers.

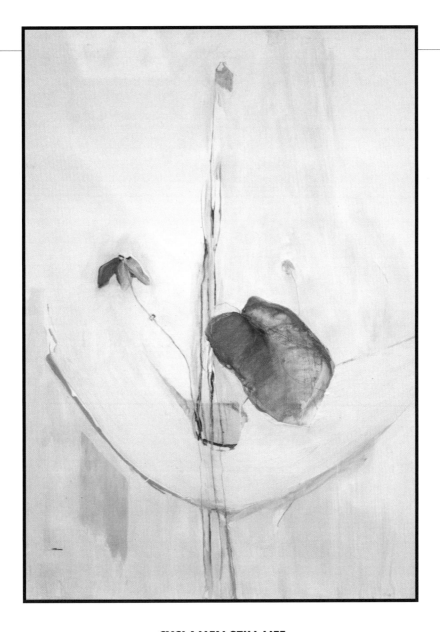

CYCLAMEN STILL LIFE

A series of huge canvases was presented to the family without warning, depicting these lovely, delicate cyclamen flowers. What had happened to the stormy skies, landscapes and images of vines?

Sometimes the tranquillity of a single flower is all that is needed to take us to another place.

July

A season of plenty – English cherries, raspberries, redcurrants and blackcurrants enhance both savoury and sweet dishes. We enjoy whole fishes pan-roasted on a vinewood open fire, fragrant herbs and field mushrooms.

THIS MONTH'S FOOD CHAMPIONS	SOURCE	CHARACTER & COMMENT	RECIPES
chillies	markets, farm shops or grow your own	hot, varied, exciting to grow	Red Snapper & Salsa
honey	markets, farm shops	floral, seasonal – just make sure it's local	July Salad and throughout the book
heritage carrots	specialist greengrocers and growers	sweet, earthy, visual, tender	July Salad
wild field mushrooms	forage	plentiful, mild, fragrant	Baked Mushrooms
nasturtium flowers and leaves	grow your own	peppery, vibrant, floral, like watercress	July Salad and throughout the coming months
marjoram flowers	grow your own	herby, floral, visual	Red Snapper
cherries	orchards, all good greengrocers	juicy, delicious, one of Europe's great treats	Cherry Clafoutis
redcurrants	all good greengrocers	tangy, bursting with flavour, visual	Baked Mushrooms
raspberries	gardens, markets, farm shops	a mouth-bursting delight	Duck with Berries, Peach Melba, Cherry Clafoutis

JULY SALAD: HERITAGE CARROTS, THYME, HONEY & ALMONDS

My daughter-in-law, Lani, is passionate about plants and now grows all sorts of specialist salads, herbs, vegetables and fruits in the polytunnel and outdoors at the vineyard. She says that home-grown heritage carrots with their strong, sweet, herbaceous, earthy flavour are beyond comparison to the standard variety we see in the shops all year round. They can be purple, white, black, red, round, oval, knobbly – you name it. This recipe celebrates the carrot itself, building on its earthy character with thyme, accentuating the natural sweetness with honey and complementing the crunchy texture with almonds.

SERVES 4–6

1kg heritage carrots, washed and cut into interesting, even pieces

2 tbsp rapeseed oil, plus extra for serving

1 tbsp thyme, chopped

2 tbsp honey

Malvern salt and freshly ground black pepper

50g flaked almonds, toasted

nasturtium flowers and leaves, to decorate

1 Preheat the oven to 200°C. Bring a large saucepan of lightly-salted water to the boil over a moderate to high heat. Cook the carrots for 3 minutes, drain, then refresh under the cold tap. Spread on kitchen paper and leave to dry.

2 Transfer the carrots to a roasting tin, add the oil, thyme and honey, then season with salt and pepper. Toss together to evenly coat all the pieces. Place the tin in the preheated oven and cook for 20 minutes. The carrots will soften but should retain a crunch.

3 Remove from the oven and allow to cool, then transfer the carrots to a serving platter, drizzle with a little extra oil, sprinkle with almonds and decorate with nasturtium flowers and leaves.

OLIVER'S TALES FROM A FORAGER'S DIARY
Seashore Delights

When I was working with Hugh Fearnley-Whittingstall down in Lyme Regis, we once caught 120 mackerel in just three hours using a few feathers off the side of a boat. Now my little boys and I go down to the Sussex coast to fish. We take a crabbing line, some bacon and a bucket. My 4-year-old had learned to tie a knot around the bacon and he dangled his line over the sea wall, into the sea. He pulled up his first crab with huge excitement (my younger son couldn't believe it either). However, both were terrified of this sea monster from the deep, so it was my job to put it safely into the bucket.

Before we had children there was a similar experience with my ever-tolerant wife. This time we were fishing with rods and she hooked a large eel. She reeled the writhing creature in and flicked it over the railing, directly into her jacket hood where it wriggled around her neck. I heard the same terrified shriek as I do from my little boys – my job to put it in the bucket.

The best part of being by the sea is the fresh air, constant movement of the water and open vista. I have foraged lots of different things from the beach, including driftwood to use as platters, pebbles for presenting seafood, sea cabbage, sea kale, sea buckthorn, sea spinach, samphire, sea purslane, dulse and grasses from the dunes – plus mussels, cockles, oysters and all sorts of fish. I am yet to catch a turbot or to gather gull's eggs (when in season) – but I am sure the day will come.

SPICY CRAB PATÉ

SERVES 4–6

300g brown and white picked crab meat

30g can of anchovy fillets, finely chopped

200g ricotta

80g celery, finely diced

80g breakfast radish, finely diced

1 lime, juice

a dash of Worcestershire sauce

a few drops of Tabasco

salt and pepper

1 small cucumber, thinly sliced

savoury biscuits, crudités and salad leaves, to serve

This yummy paté is perfect for summertime outdoor entertaining. Easy to make, the delectable spicy crab can be served as an appetizer, dinner party starter or salad-based lunch. If you are not in the mood for English wine, try a Picpoul de Pinet, a Frascati or a delicate Spanish Albariño to offset the richness of the crab.

1 For both good flavour and texture, use a mixture of brown and white crab meat. Place the crab, anchovy and ricotta into a large mixing bowl and mix together with a wooden spoon until well combined.

2 Fold in the diced celery and radish, saving a little of each to sprinkle on top, then season with lime juice, Worcestershire sauce, Tabasco, salt and pepper. Taste and then add extra seasoning if necessary – we want some real punch!

3 Arrange a ring of cucumber slices around the edge of a serving dish, then spoon the crab mixture in the centre. Sprinkle with the remaining celery and radish.

4 Chill in the fridge, then serve with crunchy savoury biscuits, crudités and salad leaves.

BAKED FIELD MUSHROOMS, BRIGHTON BLUE & REDCURRANTS

Whether you are a small child or a foraging adult, there is real joy in spotting a fairy ring of mushrooms in a dewy grass meadow and gathering them for supper. Field mushrooms start to appear early in July and this simple recipe is a perfect way to enjoy them.

SERVES 4

8 field mushrooms

3 tbsp rapeseed oil

80g redcurrant jelly

freshly ground black pepper

150g blue cheese
(Brighton Blue is our local – but any will do)

baby salad leaves and fresh redcurrants

1 Preheat the oven to 180°C. Peel the skin from the mushroom caps and pluck out the stems with your fingers. (This is a surprisingly therapeutic thing to do.) Save the skins and stems for your next vegetable stock.

2 Place the mushrooms, open side up, on a flat baking tray and drizzle with oil. Season the redcurrant jelly with black pepper and put 2 tsp on to each mushroom.

3 Slice the cheese into 8 pieces and place these on top of the jelly.

4 Bake the mushrooms in the preheated oven for about 12 minutes. The cheese should bubble and colour.

5 Serve the hot mushrooms on a bed of salad leaves and decorate with strings of fresh redcurrants. I promise you will not be disappointed.

THERE'S NOTHING LIKE A GOOD BEEF BURGER WITH TOMATO RELISH

SERVES 6

For the burgers

1kg good quality minced beef

1 onion, finely diced

1 tsp garlic powder

1 tsp English mustard powder

2 tsp chopped fresh mixed herbs

salt and freshly ground black pepper

2 egg yolks

plain flour, for dusting

For the relish

MAKES 500ML

1kg ripe tomatoes, any colour, size or shape

1 tbsp rapeseed oil

2 red onions, diced

1 fresh red chilli, chopped

2 garlic cloves, chopped

a big bunch of garden herbs, chopped

2 tbsp balsamic vinegar

4 tbsp brown sugar

salt and freshly ground black pepper

To serve

brioche rolls

lettuce

tomatoes

Alongside his key role in the vineyard, Gregory hand-rears beef cows here in West Sussex. These animals graze through the summer on the lush water meadows alongside the river Arun; the meat is hugely flavourful. The prime cuts are either sold in our restaurants or from the vineyard cellar door, but every cow we send to slaughter also creates around 1,100 burgers! Cooked on a wood fire and served with home-grown tomato relish – we are on to a winner.

1 Excluding the flour, place all the ingredients for the burgers into a large bowl, thoroughly mix together until well combined.

2 Divide the mixture into six equal portions and roll each one into a ball. Dust the work surface with a little flour and press the meat down to make thick patties. Chill these in the fridge before cooking.

3 Now make the relish. Put the oil into a large saucepan over a moderate heat, add the onion, chilli and garlic, lightly fry until the onion is soft.

4 Add the tomatoes, herbs, vinegar and sugar to the pan, seasoning generously with salt and black pepper. Bring to the boil, reduce the heat and simmer for 20 minutes, stirring occasionally to make sure it does not catch.

5 Use the relish right away or transfer to sterilized jars and store in the fridge for up to a week.

6 Make sure the barbecue is hot but not flaming. If you are using wood, it is much better to cook on the embers. Sear the burgers for 3–4 minutes on one side, then flip and cook for another 2–3 minutes on the other.

7 Serve the burgers in lightly-toasted brioche buns with salad and the tomato relish.

RICHARD'S WINES
TO SHARE AND PAIR
Our Illustrious Neighbours

Just across the lane from Nutbourne is Nyetimber, both the manor and the original vineyard. This is the brand that has put English sparkling on the global wine map – and very good it is too.

It was started by an unlikely couple named Stewart and Sandy Moss from Chicago. They had the single-minded vision to make a wine in southern England equal to the finest Champagne. They were perfectionists and did everything possible to fulfil their dream.

The house is now owned and run by the Heerema family who have continued the high standards, expanded production and established Nyetimber among the best sparkling wine in the world. All we can say is that Nutbourne shares the same valley and we were here first!

So for this month's wine pairings I am going to focus on some other great English sparklers. Try a delicate and delightful Gusbourne Blanc de Blancs with the honeyed July Salad; a more biscuity, richer Wiston Estate Cuvée with the Field Mushrooms; or, last but by no means least, the irresistible Nyetimber Rosé with the Red Snapper.

COLD DUCK BREAST, TARRAGON, BERRIES & ROCKET

Picnicking in the vines on a balmy summer's evening, eating out in the garden or just wanting something a little different to celebrate the season, this is a delightful cold summer dish to share with family or friends. Enjoy it alongside a traditional potato salad, a crisp, summer leaf salad and a glass or two of English white or rosé wine.

SERVES 6

For the dressing
100ml rapeseed oil

1 tbsp tarragon vinegar

1 tsp Dijon mustard

1 tsp soft brown sugar

1 tbsp tarragon leaves, plus extra to garnish

salt and freshly ground black pepper

1 tsp pink peppercorns

For the salad
3 duck breasts, each 180g

150g rocket leaves

200g raspberries, cut in half

150g blueberries, cut in half

1 Begin by preparing the tarragon dressing. Place the oil, vinegar, mustard, sugar and tarragon into a kitchen jug and use a stick blender to blend it together, then season with salt and pepper and stir in the pink peppercorns.

2 Score the skin side of the duck breasts by cutting parallel lines with a sharp knife. Lay the breasts on a plate, skin side up, and allow to dry for 1 hour before cooking.

3 Preheat the oven to 180°C. Place a heavy-based pan over a moderate to high heat, place the duck breasts in the pan, skin-side down, and cook, to sear and render the fat. This will take longer than you think. Use a slice to make sure the skin does not burn or stick, cook for 6–8 minutes. Flip the breasts over and seal for 1 minute on the other side.

4 Transfer the breasts and pan juices to an ovenproof dish, place in the preheated oven and cook for 6 minutes, then remove from the oven, lift out the breast and allow to cool. (Save all the duck fat and pan juices to cook some roast potatoes another time.)

5 Arrange a bed of rocket on a large serving platter. Cut the duck breasts into thin slices and arrange on the rocket. Scatter with berries, spoon over the tarragon dressing and finish with a few tarragon leaves.

WOOD-FIRE ROASTED RED SNAPPER

SERVES 4

4 whole red snappers, gutted and scaled

2 tbsp sunflower oil

salt and freshly ground black pepper

For the salsa

½ **kohlrabi,** peeled and finely diced

1 red pepper, cored and diced

1 yellow pepper, cored and diced

chervil, mint, basil, marjoram and chives (or whatever is available), chopped

1 tsp coriander seeds, crushed

100ml virgin rapeseed oil

juice of 1 lemon

To finish

lemons, cut into wedges

salad leaves

marjoram flowers

I cannot overemphasize the virtues of cooking on a wood fire. Somehow the flame and smoke bring a completely different dimension to a dish and get everyone salivating before they have even tasted it. Whole fish are particularly good cooked in this way. Here we are cooking red snapper, but trout, salmon, gurnard or bream would work in the same way. The preparation and accompaniments can be very simple: spread a vegetable salsa generously on top, offer some sourdough bread and a few salad leaves alongside, and you have a perfect meal as you sit around the fire.

1 Begin by preparing the salsa. Mix all the ingredients together in a bowl and season well with salt and pepper. Leave for a couple of hours, to infuse.

2 Build a fire of dry wood. Allow time for most of the flames to die down, leaving hot embers with just the odd pieces of burning wood.

3 Rub the snappers with sunflower oil, salt and pepper.

4 Heat a heavy pan over the fire and cook the fish for 5–6 minutes on one side, then 3–4 minutes on the other. If there is a breeze, it is advisable to put a lid or foil over the pan to make sure the heat gets through to the middle of each fish.

5 To finish, place the fish on individual serving plates, spoon some salsa along each fish and decorate with wedges of lemon, salad leaves and flowering herbs.

PEACH MELBA, HOMEMADE VANILLA ICE CREAM & NUTTY WILD

The original recipe for Peach Melba was created by Escoffier in 1892 at the Savoy Hotel, but this ice cream sundae remains a sensational summer dessert today. You could, of course, buy the ice cream, but it is actually very simple and satisfying to make your own. After that you just need some raspberries and ripe fresh peaches (before you ask, there are delicious peaches now grown in south-east England). Then we finish the dish with a splash of our very own Nutty Wild pink sparkling wine.

SERVES 6

3 ripe peaches

200g raspberries

2 tbsp agave syrup

a splash of Nutty Wild

For the ice cream

80ml milk

1 vanilla pod, split, seeds scraped out

4 egg yolks

150g caster sugar

100ml double cream

100ml plain Greek-style yoghurt

1 Start by making the ice cream. Put the milk and vanilla (pod and seeds) into a small saucepan over a moderate heat and bring up to scalding point – not boiling.

2 Place the egg yolks and sugar in a mixing bowl and, using an electric hand whisk, beat until the mixture becomes pale and doubles in volume.

3 Remove the vanilla pod from the milk. While continuing to beat the egg mixture, slowly pour in the hot milk. Once all the milk has been added, beat for a further 5 minutes.

4 In a separate bowl, whisk the double cream until it forms soft peaks, then fold in the yoghurt and whisk again for a few seconds.

5 Fold the cream and yoghurt into the egg mixture using a metal spoon, then transfer to a container and freeze overnight.

6 To assemble the sundaes, cut the peaches in half, discard the stones and cut them into wedges.

7 Using a stick blender or liquidizer, blend the raspberries with the agave syrup to form a purée.

8 Open the Nutty Wild (or equivalent), ready to finish the dessert. Drink a small glass – chef's perk!

9 When ready to serve the dessert, scoop ice cream into individual glasses, scatter with peach wedges, spoon over the raspberry purée and finish with the sparkling wine.

CHERRY CLAFOUTIS

SERVES 4

300g cherries, halved and stoned

2 tbsp brandy

1 tbsp soft brown sugar

4 sage leaves

a knob of butter

icing sugar, for dusting

clotted cream, to serve

For the batter

60g plain flour

40g ground almonds

60g caster sugar

125ml milk

125ml double cream

3 large eggs

a pinch of salt

Plump, ripe English cherries have only a short season in midsummer, so when they are around we should enjoy them in every way we can. A clafoutis is a sort of sweet Yorkshire pudding with cherries baked within it, enhanced with brandy and sage. It may seem strange to serve a hot baked pudding in the middle of July, but variety and the unexpected are important parts of culinary delight. Never be predictable!

1 Put the cherries into a bowl, add the brandy, sugar and sage. Mix together, then leave to macerate for 1 hour.

2 Preheat the oven to 190°C. Prepare an ovenproof dish by greasing it with the butter. Drain the cherries through a sieve, reserving the juice; discard the sage. Put the cherries into the dish in an even layer.

3 Use a food processor to blend all the batter ingredients together until smooth. Add the reserved liquid from the cherries and blend again.

4 Pour the batter over the cherries and place the dish in the oven for 35 minutes.

5 Remove the dish from the oven, allow to cool down a little, then dust with icing sugar and serve warm with clotted cream.

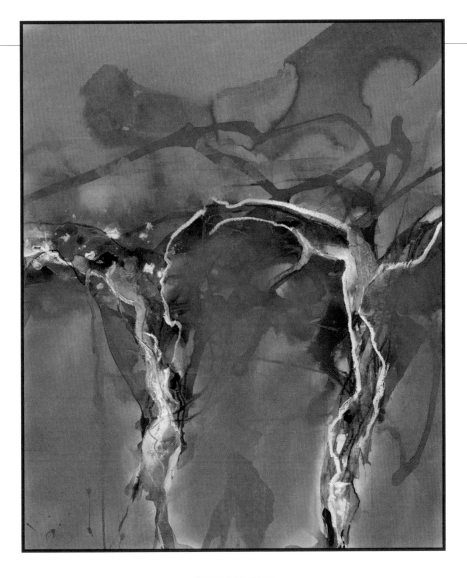

NUTTY WILD

*Bridget captures the trunk, crown and arched cordons of old vines in all their glory.
Nutty Wild is a sparkling wine made from the second pressings of Pinot Noir and
Chardonnay, fermented to just 10% alcohol. The result is a lively, expressive, fruity wine
akin to the artwork on its label.*

August

The perfume of high summer: ripe tomatoes, foraged herbs, smoky charred meats, wild berries and holiday freedom. The grape bunches are starting to swell, changing colour as their ripening begins.

THIS MONTH'S FOOD CHAMPIONS	SOURCE	CHARACTER & COMMENT	RECIPES
tomatoes	gardens, markets, farm shops	full-flavoured, fruity, perfumed	August Salad, Gazpacho, Soggy Bread Salad
basil	all good greengrocers – or grow your own beneath the tomatoes	fragrant, sweet, spicy herb	Gazpacho
apple marigold	garden centres, grow your own	herbaceous, citrus and apple	August Salad
puffball	forage in pastureland	delicate, fleshy, tender	Soggy Bread Salad
lamb's kidneys	good butchers	smooth, lamby, addictive	Lamb's Kidneys
cucumbers	British – all good greengrocers	crisp, cool and uplifting	Chicken Salad
grouse	shoots and specialist game butchers	rich, succulent, gamey	Moorland Grouse
mulberries	rare – gardens and parks	wonderful, like no other	Pavlova
elderberries	forage in the countryside	spiky, tart, colourful	Moorland Grouse, Bramble Fool
edible flowers: pelargonium, marigold, fennel and clover	gardens and in the wild	visual, tangy, aromatic	Salmon, Pavlova and Bramble Fool

GIANT PUFFBALL WITH
SOGGY BREAD & TOMATO SALAD

SERVES 6

1 giant puffball

salt and freshly ground black pepper

125g butter

2 garlic cloves, crushed

For the soggy bread and tomato salad

3 slices of stale bread, cut into chunks

600g ripe tomatoes, cut into chunks

a good bunch of basil leaves

3 tbsp of virgin rapeseed oil

Finding a puffball is discovering real treasure, especially when you know how wonderful it is going to be when cooked with butter and garlic. They appear out of nowhere: large, gleaming white balls sticking out of the grass after rainfall on open pastureland. The puffball itself has a tender, meaty flesh with a rich nutty flavour. Where 'Soggy Bread Salad' comes from, I don't know. Bridget hates to throw anything away (quite rightly) and in midsummer she makes this salad to use up stale bread and maximize the juices of overripe tomatoes. This may not sound that good but is actually completely yummy, perfect with the fried giant puffball. A great treat like this deserves some good wine. At home we would choose our barrel-fermented Chardonnay for its honeyed buttery quality but the same can be found in a decent Mâcon, Saint-Véran or Montagny from Burgundy.

1 Prepare the salad by tossing all the ingredients together in a large bowl; season with salt and plenty of freshly ground black pepper. Leave it for an hour to develop flavour and become soggy.

2 Cut the puffball into even slices and season with salt and pepper.

3 Heat a large, heavy-based pan over a moderate heat. Melt about one third of the butter in the pan, add the garlic and fry for 1 minute.

4 Add the puffball slices to the pan and toss them: the butter will instantly be absorbed, so add more butter while continuing to cook and toss the mushroom for no more than 3 or 4 minutes

5 Serve immediately with the Soggy Bread & Tomato Salad.

OLIVER'S TALES FROM A FORAGER'S DIARY
The Giant Puffball

I am always on the lookout for something edible. One early misty August morning, driving my van through the countryside towards London, I spotted a big white blob in a field. I instantly knew what it was, so I pulled over at the first opportunity, clambered through the hedge and walked to the middle of the field to forage a magnificent brilliant white mushroom. As I picked it up, I heard a farmer's voice shouting from the other end of the field. I probably should have stopped to politely explain why I was trespassing, but instead I put the giant puffball under my arm like a rugby ball and ran as fast as I could, back through the hedge and into the van. When I had safely escaped, I looked back to realise it was only a solitary dog walker shouting after his dog, not an angry farmer at all.

TOMATO GAZPACHO

SERVES 4

8 plum tomatoes

1 small red onion, cut in half

6 basil leaves, shredded

2 tbsp olive oil

1 tbsp balsamic vinegar

6 drops of Tabasco

salt and freshly ground black pepper

a little caster sugar

basil leaves and viola petals, to decorate

There are two key secrets to making this exquisite, refreshing, chilled summer soup. The first is to use ripe, sweet tomatoes – not always easy to buy but, kept out of the fridge for a few days, tomatoes can be ripened at home. The second thing is not to use a food processor or liquidizer: a fine gazpacho is made by pounding or grating the ingredients. This timeless recipe is lighter and more refreshing than most. For me, nothing could be more delightful.

1 Cut the tomatoes in half and remove the green core but nothing else. We include the pips.

2 There is no need to blanch and peel the tomatoes. Using the coarse side of a traditional grater over a deep bowl, grate the tomatoes: the flesh and juice will separate from the skins. Discard the skins.

3 Grate the red onion into the tomato mix in the same way.

4 Add the shredded basil leaves, olive oil, balsamic vinegar and Tabasco, then season well with salt, pepper and a little sugar.

5 Stir the mixture together, then place in the fridge to macerate and chill.

6 Serve in chilled bowls, decorated with extra basil leaves and viola petals.

CUCUMBER & CHILLI CHICKEN SALAD

This is a perfect picnic dish, simple to prepare in advance and easy to eat cross-legged on the grass in the shade of a vine or a big tree.

1 Put the chicken thighs into a deep pan and pour over enough water to cover. Add the onion, parsley and thyme, season with salt and pepper, place over a moderate heat, bring to the boil, simmer for 10 minutes.

2 Lift out a piece of chicken to check that it is cooked through. When satisfied, drain through a sieve. When the chicken is cold enough to handle, take the meat off the bone and cut into strips.

3 Mix the chilli, lime juice, coriander, oil and syrup together, season with salt. Pour this mixture over the chicken, transfer to the fridge to chill and infuse the flavours.

4 Peel, quarter and deseed the cucumbers and cut into chunks. Gently combine the cucumber and crème fraiche with the chicken. Transfer to a serving dish, finish with lettuce leaves, extra chilli rings, lime strings, coriander leaves, fennel flowers and marigold petals

SERVES 6

500g free-range chicken thighs

1 onion, chopped

parsley and thyme

salt and freshly ground black pepper

1 red chilli, finely diced, with a few rings reserved to decorate

2 limes, zest (in fine strips) and juice

a small bunch of coriander, chopped, with a few leaves reserved to decorate

2 tbsp rapeseed oil

1 tbsp maple syrup

2 standard cucumbers or 6 small ones

2 tbsp crème fraiche

marigold petals and fennel flowers, to decorate

TIP After cooking the chicken, save the stock for another recipe. We always have a meat or vegetable stock in the fridge: it is the starting point for your next creation.

BARBECUED LAMB'S KIDNEYS, FRESH MINT JELLY

It is surprising who likes offal – more people than you might think – and it is all too rarely served. This preparation is a real treat for those who enjoy grilled meat cooked on the fire complemented by a natural, tangy handmade jelly. The underripe apples are a great way to set the jelly as they provide natural pectin. Don't be tempted to remove the pips or core: this is where most of the pectin is stored.

SERVES 4

400g lamb's kidneys

1 tbsp rapeseed oil

salt and freshly ground black pepper

For the mint jelly

a bunch of fresh mint

2 hard underripe apples

250ml water

2 tbsp cider vinegar

250g caster sugar

1 Begin by making the mint jelly. This can be made well in advance and stored in the fridge for several weeks. Strip two-thirds of the mint leaves from their stalks and chop the apples into pieces – core, pips and all. Place these in a blender with the water and vinegar and blitz to a purée.

2 Transfer the mixture to a heavy-bottomed pan and bring to the boil over a moderate heat. Remove the pan from the heat and allow to steep for 1 hour.

3 Break up the cooked apple with a spoon, then transfer the mixture into a fine sieve set over a jug or bowl; allow 30 minutes for the juice to drain out.

4 Discard the cooked apple and mint. Place a saucer in the freezer, to chill. Put the juice back into a pan, add the sugar and bring to the boil over a moderate heat. Cook for a few minutes, then test the consistency by placing a few drops on to the chilled saucer to assess the set. Cook for a little longer, if required.

5 When the jelly has cooled, shred the remaining mint leaves and add them, stirring gently. Transfer to the fridge.

6 Prepare the kidneys by removing the skin and snipping out the hard white core using a pair of kitchen scissors. Toss the kidneys in oil, season, skewer on to kebab sticks and leave to marinate for 30 minutes.

7 Prepare a hot but not flaming barbecue. Cook the kidney kebabs evenly on both sides. They should be seared on the outside but remain pink in the centre.

8 Serve with a spoonful of the Fresh Mint Jelly on the side.

POACHED SALMON WITH WATERCRESS VICHYSSOISE

SERVES 4

4 pieces of salmon, each 120g

a few fennel fronds

½ onion, chopped

50g jar keta caviar (salmon roe)

fennel flowers

For the vichyssoise

2 tbsp rapeseed oil

I large leek (300g), washed, trimmed and chopped

200g potatoes, peeled and diced

salt and freshly ground black pepper

300ml water

80ml milk

80ml crème fraiche

1 lemon, zest and juice

80g watercress, chopped

This is a fantastic summer main course: delicately poached salmon topped with keta caviar and served on a chilled Watercress Vichyssoise. Vichyssoise is a cold summer soup made from leek and potato; the addition of watercress gives it a lovely fresh colour and peppery taste. We first enjoyed this dish on a flaming hot August day, sheltering in the shade of the mulberry tree in our garden. We were drinking our own delicate crisp Ten.Five Chardonnay. Bliss!

1 Make the vichyssoise. Put the oil into a heavy-based pan over a low to moderate heat. Add the leeks and potatoes and fry for 5 minutes, stirring frequently. Season well with salt and pepper.

2 Add the water to the pan, bring to the boil, then reduce the heat and simmer for 20 minutes.

3 Allow the mixture to cool a little, then transfer to a food processor and blitz until smooth.

4 Stir in the milk, crème fraiche, lemon zest and juice, and the watercress. Transfer to a large jug and chill in the fridge.

5 Preheat the oven to 180°C. Put the salmon in a shallow ovenproof dish. Arrange the fennel fronds and onion around, add water to not quite cover the fish, season with salt and pepper and cover with foil.

6 Place the salmon in the oven and cook for 15 minutes. Remove from the oven and allow the fish to go cold in the cooking liquor. Chill in the fridge until ready to serve.

7 Pour about 2cm of vichyssoise into individual bowls, place a piece of salmon on top, then finish with keta caviar and fennel flowers.

AUGUST SALAD: HERITAGE TOMATOES, BURRATA, APPLE MARIGOLD & BALSAMIC PEARLS

Garry, Jenny and their family have been specialist tomato growers in our village for over 30 years. Restaurants, delicatessens and specialist food stores throughout the country now make a feature of Nutbourne tomatoes. Their growing season runs from April right through to late October, but August is really the best month for ripe, sweet, flavoursome Sussex-grown tomatoes. In this recipe we combine them with the appley, tart, floral flavour of apple marigold leaves, pearls of white balsamic vinegar and the creamy richness of burrata cheese.

SERVES 6

For the balsamic pearls

300ml rapeseed oil (can be reused)

80ml white balsamic vinegar

½ tsp agar-agar

For the salad

600g assorted heritage tomatoes

rock salt and freshly ground black pepper

A drizzle of virgin rapeseed oil (or olive oil)

1 burrata cheese

small bunch of apple marigold leaves

1 Begin by preparing the balsamic pearls. Put the oil in an open bowl, place in the freezer and deep-chill for at least 3 hours.

2 Put the vinegar into a small pan, whisk in the agar-agar and allow to soak for 2 minutes, then place the pan over a gentle heat and bring to the boil.

3 Wait for 3 minutes then, using a syringe (or very small spoon), squeeze droplets of the vinegar into the deep-chilled oil. The balsamic will instantly gel into perfectly round pearls that provide little starbursts of flavour. (The pearls can be stored in their oil for many months.)

4 Next, prepare the salad. I always like to vary the cutting of the tomatoes – some quartered, some sliced and some left whole. Gently toss the cut tomatoes with salt, pepper and a little oil.

5 Drain the burrata and place it in the centre of a serving dish. Casually arrange the tomatoes around the cheese and add small sprigs of marigold leaves.

6 Lift the balsamic pearls out of the oil using a slotted spoon and dot them across the salad. Very simple, and very delicious!

MOORLAND GROUSE WITH ELDERBERRIES, TARRAGON & MUSHROOMS

SERVES 2

2 moorland grouse, plucked

1 tbsp rapeseed oil

20g butter

salt and freshly ground black pepper

game chips, to serve

For the sauce

80g penny bun mushrooms or similar, sliced

80ml port

juice of 1 lemon

a few sprigs of tarragon, stalks removed, chopped, with a few whole leaves reserved

20g elderberries

TIP There will be leftover grouse, jus and mushrooms, so the following day you can enjoy stripping the remaining flesh off the carcass, boiling the bones with some onion and bay to make a sensational game stock, then bringing it all together in a mouth-watering grouse and wild mushroom risotto.

I remember the first time I ordered grouse in a rather exclusive London restaurant specializing in game. A traditional chef-patron ran the establishment. He insisted on taking the orders himself before returning to his kitchen to cook. On choosing new-season grouse, the question was put, did I want it 'bloody or ruined?' I think there was only one right answer and, sure enough, the rare-roasted bird was out of this world. I have never forgotten it. I appreciate that readers are unlikely to cook grouse very often but, if you do get the chance, I thought it would be helpful to offer some guidance. Prepared carefully with the delectable addition of elderberries, wild mushrooms and tarragon, this is a real treat.

---

1 Preheat the oven to 200°C. It is best to cook grouse whole, with the offal still inside. Heat the oil and butter together in a heavy-based pan over a moderate heat, season the birds well with salt and pepper, place in the hot pan and brown the skin on all sides.

2 Immediately transfer the hot birds to a roasting tin, place in the oven and cook for 10–12 minutes.

3 Meanwhile, prepare the sauce. Add the mushrooms to the hot pan, cook them quickly, then lift them out and keep warm. Add to the pan the port, lemon juice, chopped tarragon and elderberries, boil rapidly for 2 minutes, then taste and season.

4 Remove the grouse from the oven, cover to keep warm and allow to rest for 10 minutes before carving.

5 Now comes the skilled bit: remove the breasts and a section of leg meat from the bone, scoop out the offal and find the liver and the heart. Arrange these prize components of the bird on individual plates, add the mushrooms, spoon over the sauce and dot with a few tarragon leaves. Serve some crisp game chips alongside.

**RICHARD'S WINES
TO SHARE AND PAIR
The Six Senses of Wine**

We can use all six senses to appreciate wine. Begin by the touch of the bottle: chilled, dewy, weighty. Enjoy the sound of the cork popping and the gentle cascade into a glass. Observe the sight of the fine shaped bottle, the beautiful label, the clarity and colour of the liquid. Lift the glass to your nose to smell it: breathe in the aroma, take stock of all the subtleties; taste the wine slowly, carefully,

in all parts of your mouth, capturing the acidity, tannins, body, fruit and balance. Finally, allow your emotion to fill your head and soul with nothing but the amazing experience of this thing called wine.

I am tempted by a Sicilian Grillo white with the August Salad: inexpensive lovely summer drinking. Then for the grouse we need to go the whole hog: it has to be a fine Pauillac such as Chateau Batailley or a Saint-Julien such as Réserve de Léoville-Barton.

Lastly, it is our own Nutbourne Hedgerow I would choose with the two quintessentially English fruity puddings.

MULBERRY PAVLOVA

If you are lucky enough to have a mulberry tree in your garden, or you have access to one, it is the most exquisite, uniquely flavoured berry. In our opinion, mulberries beat all the other summer fruits for intensity, juiciness and sheer indulgence. Bridget harvests our big tree day after day, usually around the first two weeks of August. She wears a dedicated outfit covered with bright purple stains – plus the occasional (at first alarming) red splodge will appear on her head! The fruits really are very juicy. We put some mulberries in the freezer, cook some to make a syrup and most meals will feature a mulberry dessert. This simple pavlova is the perfect vehicle to enjoy them. As for wine, rosé bubbles are surely the answer – well chilled, fun, fizzy, with ample fruit and zing.

SERVES 6–8

oil, for greasing

6 free-range egg whites

300g caster sugar

a pinch of salt

1 tbsp cornflour

1 tbsp white wine vinegar

250ml double cream

400g mulberries, dusted with some icing sugar to bring out the juices

pelargonium petals and fennel flowers

TIP This recipe uses the whites only from six eggs; save four of the yolks to make the custard for Bramble Fool (page 130).

1 Preheat the oven to 130°C. Use a large dinner plate to mark out a big circle on baking paper. Roughly trim the paper and place it on a baking sheet brushed with oil.

2 Use a standing mixer to whisk the egg whites to stiff peaks. Continue to whisk and slowly add the sugar, a spoonful at a time.

3 When all the sugar has been incorporated, beat in the salt, cornflour and vinegar. Continue to whisk for another couple of minutes until the meringue has a shiny high gloss.

4 Spoon or pipe the meringue on to the circle of baking paper. Start around the edge, then work into the middle to form a solid base about 3cm deep.

5 Bake in the oven for 1 hour. Then, without opening the door, turn the oven off and allow the pavlova to slowly cool inside.

6 Assemble the dessert. Whip the double cream to a firm but not dry consistency, spread a generous layer on to the meringue, then top with the sugared mulberries and edible flowers.

BRAMBLE, ELDERBERRY & RED CLOVER FOOL

SERVES 6

300g wild blackberries

60g elderberries,
stalks removed

2 tbsp caster sugar

For the custard

500ml whole milk

200ml double cream

½ vanilla pod,
seeds scraped out

100g caster sugar

4 egg yolks

3 tbsp cornflour

To finish

250ml double cream

4 red clover flowers

This is a dessert celebrating the countryside in August. Our vineyard is bordered by bramble hedges full of succulent, tangy wild blackberries; the elder trees have ripened clusters of peppery sweet elderberries; and the red clover growing among the wildflower strips is an irresistible colour and lends a little herbaceous finish to this glorious dessert.

1 Mix the berries and sugar together and leave in the fridge to steep for a couple of hours.

2 Prepare the custard. Put the milk and cream into a heavy-based saucepan over a moderate heat. Add the vanilla seeds and pod to the pan. Bring up to scalding point but do not boil.

3 Whisk the egg yolks, sugar and cornflour together in a heatproof bowl. Pour in the hot milk and cream while continuing to whisk.

4 When the mixture is well combined, place the bowl over the second pan of simmering water over a gentle heat. Continue to stir for another 5 minutes, until the custard is smooth and very thick. Discard the vanilla pod and transfer the custard to the fridge to chill.

5 Whip the second quantity of cream until firm, spoon the custard, fruit mixture and whipped cream separately into a serving dish, then gently swirl them together. Sprinkle the top with tiny petals of red clover.

SUSSEX DOWNS & HEDGEROWS

This hot, summery painting was inspired by the changing patterns of fields, hedges and woodland across the Sussex countryside. Bridget set her easel high on the South Downs to see the tapestry of colours and shapes below her.

This image is featured on the label of Nutbourne Hedgerow wine, an off-dry, aromatic wine that conjures up the essence of summertime hedgerow fruits.

AUTUMN

The weather is still fine, the garden has plenty of flowers, hedgerows are abundant with wild fruits and the grapes are ripening on the vines, but now there is mist in the early morning, temperatures drop in the late afternoon and there is more moisture in the air – summer has run its course and autumn is on its way.

This is surely the most exciting period of the year for a winemaker, and maybe for a chef as well. For wine producers the grape harvest is the pinnacle of eleven months' labour nurturing the vines. For the chef there is an abundance of big wholesome cooking to explore.

THE VINEYARD

Daylight is just breaking on a late September morning; mist over the vineyard, peaceful and beautiful; the line of the South Downs peaking high on the horizon, catching first glimpses of watery sun. The vines look magnificent. All is prepared for the onslaught of the day ahead, orderly rows stretching south, laden with red, golden and green bunches awaiting their destiny. For Gregory and me, there is nothing better than the early start before a busy harvest day – a curious mixture of calm, anticipation and excitement before the mass of pickers arrive and the sounds of tractors, instructions and background chatter kick in.

Nutbourne is a hive of activity at this time of year. The different grape varieties are checked daily. As the crop ripens the sugar levels rise and the acidity reduces. However, we want the best of both worlds – high sugar to transform into alcohol but also good acidity for strong fruit flavours, freshness and character. We are looking for a balanced 'sweet spot' to trigger the decision to pick the crop. A harvest day requires an early start. Local people from all walks of life arrive to experience the joys of vendange. We joke that if there are 30 pickers the first day, 20 will return the second and by day three we will have whittled it down to a hard core of around 15. It may not be that bad, but picking grapes all day long is not for the faint-hearted. The grape bunches are picked by hand and placed into boxes for the three brothers to collect, with Dad backing a tractor down each row.

We harvest for up to 10 days, spread over four weeks, as different grape varieties ripen at differing times. We are also in the hands of the weather. Rain doesn't just make picking unpleasant, it could dilute the end wine with water. By the end of October the vines have been denuded and quickly start to shed their leaves for a well-deserved period of winter rest.

THE WINERY

The winery comes into its own in the autumn. On a good harvest day we will process over 8 tons of fruit in two or three separate press loads. Gregory leads the winemaking, working well into the night, but the adrenaline of the season means that he will still be the first on site the following morning. The process of fermenting grape juice into wine is ancient, natural and simple. We are great believers that good wine is made in the vineyard not the winery. In the flowery language of wine tasting, wines are described in many fabulous ways – peppercorns and leather, ripe damsons and tobacco, or freshly mown grass with hints of gooseberries. There are no restrictions on sensory descriptions, but the one thing no one says is 'it tastes like grape juice' – and that is simply because it doesn't! The process of fermenting grapes into wine, known to be at least 6,000 years old, is a miraculous transformation.

For white wines the grapes are pressed as whole bunches but we use only the juice. With the addition of yeast, this ferments into wine. For red wine we use the berries off their stems, keeping the skins and pips as essential parts of the process until they are sieved out at the end. Each tank is tasted and tested daily to monitor progress. White wine is best fermented 'slow and cool' to preserve the subtle fruit flavours, whilst red wine can afford to be 'hot and swift', capturing the full spectrum of the sun-ripened berries.

As autumn draws on, the wines begin to 'finish' as all the sugar in the grapes has fermented into alcohol. Some is then transferred to oak barrels to mature whilst other wines remain on the lees in their tanks to develop over the winter. The family meets for a special celebration of the vendange, eats too much, drinks some of the new wine comparing it to older vintages from the cellar, and debates the success of our labours.

HARVEST MORALE AND BRIDGET'S BIRTHDAY

We have the main event of the grape harvest, which is celebrated in all winemaking regions of the world. Plentiful picnic lunches to eat on the go when time allows, wholesome hot meals at the end of the day, and an endless supply of in-between morale-boosting treats are all essential for a successful harvest season. In our family there are also multiple autumn birthdays to celebrate – little Iris and Imogen, two of the brothers, and in mid-October comes Bridget's birthday. This is a great excuse for family and friends to descend on Nutbourne to party.

In my childhood, Bonfire Night was another great time for family parties with outdoor cooking, mulled wine, treacle toffee and, of course, fireworks. Nowadays this seems to have been replaced by Halloween. The littlies love it, lots of dressing up and loads of really unhealthy sweeties!

AUTUMNAL COOKING

There is no better season of diverse ingredients and culinary opportunities. As the season changes, so does our cooking style. It is a time for bolder flavours, more wholesome dishes, game birds, wild mushrooms and other woodland treats, orchard fruits and an abundance of home-grown vegetables.

Once again, we champion specific ingredients each month and then unashamedly use them as much as possible. This is what seasonal cooking is all about: if you have an oversupply of apples, you give some to your neighbours but also find 10 different ways to incorporate them into your cooking.

It is still a great time for local vegetables, whether you grow your own or visit a farmers' market. Try the Onion Squash Gnocchi or Stuffed Aubergine recipes. The range of marrows, beans and the spectrum of fresh mushrooms is incredible. I can recommend the Wild Mushroom & Hazelnut Soufflé with a commitment to cook a plant-based dish at least once a week.

A change in the weather does not stop my family from wanting to cook and eat outside whenever possible, such as hispi cabbage with fallow deer cooked on an open fire, or red gurnard roasted in the wood-fired oven and heritage pumpkins chargrilled out of doors. The hedgerows and orchards are abundant with fruits, nuts and berries to make amazing puddings. Our Apple, Plum & Frangipane Slice or the Quince Treacle Tart are well worth exploring.

Finally, it is a traditional time of year to cook some larder provisions. Try to get your hands on some medlars to make the richest jelly you have ever tasted or some sloes to make your own sloe gin truffles.

A season of change, diversity and plenty.

THE AUTUMN PALETTE

For some autumn is a melancholy time, ever-shorter days, first frosts with winter looming ahead, bleak and long. But the changing colours are an inspiration for all of us and, if you are an artist, there is inspiration everywhere you look across the landscape: the skies, the fields, the forests or just the garden leaves turning vibrant, dramatic, determined to finish their year with a lasting impression of splendour.

September

An abundance of squashes, beans, mushrooms and orchard fruits. The first hint of a chill in the air sending the signal to gather, forage, dry and bottle for the leaner months ahead.

THIS MONTH'S FOOD CHAMPIONS	SOURCE	CHARACTER & COMMENT	RECIPES
beans: runners, broad, string or fine	all good greengrocers, or grow your own	nutritious, mild, a great carrier for other flavours	September Salad
marrows and squashes	all good greengrocers, or grow your own	creamy, wholesome, delicate	Tempura Marrow, Onion Squash Gnocchi, September Salad
sea kale, sea lettuce and seaweeds	forage on the seashore	savoury, salty, intense	Seashore Soup
chanterelles	forage in woodland	delicate, buttery, complex	Onion Squash Gnocchi
apples	orchards, farm shops, all good greengrocers	varied, lasting, fresh, fleshy	Pork Tenderloin, Spatchcocked Chicken, Apple Frangipane
brambles	forage from hedgerows	tart, tangy, textured – don't confuse with cultivated blackberries	Spatchcocked Chicken, Blackberry Cobbler
pears and plums	orchards, farm shops, all good greengrocers	flavoursome, sweet, tangy, perfumed	Blackberry Cobbler, Apple Frangipane
sage	all good greengrocers, or grow your own	distinctive, herby, medicinal	Onion Squash Gnocchi, Pork Tenderloin
grapes	vineyards	a spectrum of flavours and styles	Wine!

TEMPURA MARROW WITH SWEET CHILLI

SERVES 4–8

1 medium-sized marrow

100g tempura batter mix

about 80ml soda water

1l sunflower oil, for frying (this can be reused)

radish slices and flat-leaf parsley or coriander, to serve

For the chilli dipping sauce

2 red chillies, roughly chopped

1 garlic clove, roughly chopped

3cm piece of root ginger, peeled and roughly chopped

50ml water

50ml white wine vinegar

150g caster sugar

½ tsp salt

TIP If you don't have a thermometer, check the temperature of the oil by cooking a small piece of bread: it should fry quickly, but without burning.

We have all enjoyed battered calamari, especially on Mediterranean holidays, but I was hugely impressed when Oliver introduced me to this tempura-battered marrow. Serve it as a snack to accompany a crisp, fragrant Provence rosé.

1 Begin with the chilli dipping sauce. Put the chilli, garlic, ginger, water and vinegar into a liquidizer, blitz for a few seconds.

2 Transfer the mixture to a small pan set over a moderate heat. Stir in the sugar and salt, bring up to the boil, reduce the heat and simmer for 10 minutes. Set aside and leave to cool.

3 Peel the marrow, cut it in half, remove the seeds, then slice crossways into half-moon pieces. Whisk the soda water into the batter mix to create a smooth coating consistency.

4 Heat the oil in a heavy-bottomed saucepan over a moderate heat to a temperature of 325°C. Dip the marrow pieces in the batter to coat evenly. Deep fry a few pieces at a time, for 2–3 minutes, turning occasionally with a slotted spoon.

5 Once cooked, lift out the marrow and drain on kitchen paper.

6 Serve piping hot, finished with radish, parsley and the chilli sauce.

SEASHORE SOUP

When I first took my future wife down to my parents' cottage on the Sussex coast, we went on an inevitable family beach walk. Along with gentle quizzing about this and that, Bridget proceeded to gather handfuls of sea kale and then found some seaweed as well. When we got back she volunteered to make soup and cooked a delicious seashore concoction which my dad, in particular, adored. He repeatedly told this tale to anyone who would listen for the rest of his days. He would add what a talented and special girl she was and how lucky his wayward son was to have met her.

SERVES 4

40g butter

600g sea kale, washed, de-stalked and shredded

200g sea lettuce or dulse, washed and shredded

1 tbsp flour

600ml water

600ml milk

2 lemons, zest and juice

freshly ground white pepper

200ml cream

crusty bread and butter, to serve

1 Melt the butter in a large heavy-based pan over a moderate heat. Add the kale and sea lettuce and cook for 5 minutes, to soften.

2 Stir in the flour and cook for another 2 minutes.

3 Add the water, milk, lemon zest and juice, season with plenty of pepper, bring to the boil, then reduce the heat and simmer for 20 minutes.

4 Taste the soup for further seasoning and check that the leaves are tender. Stir in the cream and serve hot with crusty bread and butter.

SEPTEMBER SALAD: MIXED GARDEN BEANS, BUTTERNUT & SEEDS WITH OAT MILK YOGHURT DRESSING

Our veg garden is dripping with different types of beans hanging on their hazelwood trellis. Use whatever beans you have for this delightful September Salad – the more variety, the better. We combine the beans with roasted butternut squash, together with sunflower, pumpkin and linseeds for interest and texture. The dressing is made with vegan oat milk yoghurt and English mustard powder, adding a little richness and bite.

SERVES 4–6

1kg mixed beans: runner, broad, string, black or French

1 butternut squash, peeled, cored and cut into chunks

80g mixed seeds: sunflower, pumpkin, fennel or linseeds

2 tbsp rapeseed oil

1 tbsp honey

salt and freshly ground black pepper

For the dressing

250g oat milk yoghurt

1 tsp English mustard powder

2 tsp cider vinegar

1 tbsp honey

To finish

nasturtium leaves and petals

1 Preheat the oven to 180°C. Put a large pan of lightly-salted water over a moderate heat and bring up to the boil. Cook each type for 3–5 minutes, then lift out with a slotted spoon and plunge straight into a bowl of iced water to arrest the cooking and preserve the colour. Transfer to a colander to drain.

2 Mix the butternut squash and the seeds with the oil and honey in an ovenproof dish. Season to taste with salt and pepper.

3 Place in the oven and cook for 15–20 minutes (or use an air fryer). Test the butternut to see that it is soft right through, then remove from the oven and allow it to cool in its juices.

4 Make the dressing. Place all the ingredients in a bowl and use a hand whisk or stick blender to mix until well combined.

5 Transfer the beans to a salad bowl, arrange the butternut on top, scraping all the seeds and juices from the cooking dish, then drizzle with the dressing and decorate with nasturtium leaves and petals.

OLIVER'S TALES FROM A FORAGER'S DIARY
September, Walking the Dogs

Dad regularly does an evening walk with Rusty, Chip and Rufus, come rain or shine. It is his time to enjoy the peace of the countryside on his own. However, September walks are more about feasting than foraging: he will return with pink lips and fingers, having enjoyed hedgerow blackberries, elderberries, the odd wild apple and more.

The dogs have other interests in mind and, as all dog owners will know, man's best friend is obedient, loyal and well-behaved until he or she suddenly isn't. The scent of a deer can turn a well-behaved dog back into a wild hunting predator in a second. We give praise and treats to the first dog to respond to our urgent shouts and whistles. (Well, eventually they all have to get the treat or else it would be unfair.) But let's not be naive about the natural instincts of our loving pups.

MONKFISH & CHARD 'EN CROUTE'

SERVES 4

600g monkfish tail, filleted by your fishmonger

salt and freshly ground black pepper

6–8 chard leaves

160g ready-rolled puff pastry

1 egg, lightly beaten

40g black sesame seeds

For the butter sauce

2 tbsp white wine

1 tbsp lemon juice

a pinch of saffron

1 tsp caster sugar

100g butter, cut into small pieces

To finish

herb oil

marigold petals

TIP By weight, saffron is the most expensive product in the world – but you don't need much for this dish.

This is such an original and exotic creation of Oliver's: the monkfish tail roasts beautifully in its pastry ring and is perfectly complemented by the bilious saffron butter sauce. For me, this is a dish that cries out for fine, 'barrel-fermented' Chardonnay wine. We have been trialling barrel ferments at Nutbourne. This is an ancient natural process where newly pressed grape juice, together with some active yeast, is put into oak barrels and simply left for nine months to ferment and develop. It is our answer to the fine white wines of Burgundy, Meursault or Puligny-Montrachet in particular, though I must confess that, with their 2,000 years' experience advantage, we still have some way to go.

1 Cut the monkfish tail into two long strips, season with salt and pepper and place on to kitchen paper to dry.

2 Heat a pan of lightly-salted water over a moderate heat. Blanch the chard leaves, a couple at a time, for one minute. Rinse under the cold tap and smooth out on a board, cut out the stalks, then lay out a square of overlapping leaves measuring approximately 20cm x 20cm.

3 Place the fish fillets facing in opposite ways, across the chard. Wrap the chard tightly around the fish, to create a log shape. Wrap it in kitchen paper, to absorb as much moisture as possible.

4 Cut a 20cm x 20cm square of ready-rolled puff pastry and place it on the work surface. Remove the paper from the chard-wrapped fish, place it on the pastry and wrap, sealing the join with a few dabs of water.

5 Brush the pastry log with beaten egg, then roll it in sesame seeds. Cut it into 4 even pieces and place these, cut side up, on a baking tin lined with baking paper. Keep in the fridge until you are ready to cook.

6 Prepare the butter sauce. Place the wine, lemon juice, saffron and sugar in a small pan over a gentle heat. Season well with salt and pepper and bring up to the boil.

7 Cut the butter into small pieces and place in a bowl, pour over the hot liquid and whisk together. Keep warm or reheat over a bain-marie when required.

8 Remove the fish 'en croute' from the fridge 10 minutes before cooking. Preheat the oven to 180°C and cook for 8–10 minutes.

9 Serve immediately on individual plates, on a pool of the butter sauce. Sprinkle with marigold petals and a few droplets of oil.

ONION SQUASH GNOCCHI, SPINACH & CHANTERELLES

There are days when we really don't need to eat meat, fish, potatoes or any other conventional meal. September gives us a lovely variety of squashes and wild mushrooms to feast upon. Homemade gnocchi with the tang of spinach, the nutty crunch of pine nuts and gorgeous new-season chanterelle mushrooms is an irresistible combination.

SERVES 4

80g butter

a few sage leaves

40g pine nuts

100g chanterelle mushrooms

150g baby spinach leaves

For the gnocchi

600g onion squash, peeled, deseeded and cut into chunks

1 garlic clove, crushed

1 tbsp rapeseed oil

salt and freshly ground black pepper

1 large egg

80g plain flour, plus extra for dusting

60g hard cheese, finely grated

½ tsp ground nutmeg

TIP An onion squash is so-called because of its shape rather than its flavour. If you cannot find one, substitute butternut squash.

1 Preheat the oven to 180°C. To make the gnocchi, put the squash and garlic into an ovenproof dish, coat with oil and season with salt and pepper. Roast in the oven for 25 minutes.

2 Transfer the cooked squash to a food processor and blitz to a purée.

3 Put the purée into a large mixing bowl, make a well in the middle and stir in the egg. Mix the flour with the grated cheese and nutmeg, sprinkle about half of this mixture into the bowl, then knead to form a dough. Keep kneading, adding more of the flour mixture until it is dry and firm.

4 Dust the work surface with flour and form the dough into cylindrical lengths, then cut these into 3cm pieces.

5 Bring a large pan of salted water to the boil over a moderate heat. Cook the gnocchi, a few at a time, by gently lowering them into the water with a slotted spoon. When they are cooked, after approximately 2 minutes per batch, they will float to the surface and should be removed using the slotted spoon. Set aside and allow to cool.

6 To finish the dish, heat the butter in a heavy-based pan over a moderate heat. Fry the pine nuts and sage leaves for less than a minute, lift them out of the pan and set aside.

7 Add the mushrooms to the pan and stir-fry for 2–3 minutes. Now add the gnocchi and cook for a further 2–3 minutes, to heat through. Finally, stir in the spinach leaves and cook for a minute, until they have wilted.

8 Toss the mixture together, then serve immediately with the crispy sage leaves and pine nuts on top. It is a complete meal in one dish.

CHARGRILLED PORK TENDERLOIN, COX'S APPLES & SAGE

SERVES 4

600g pork tenderloin, cut into 8 pieces

salt and freshly ground black pepper

2 tbsp rapeseed oil

red onion, sliced

a dash of cider vinegar

2 Cox's apples, quartered, cored and sliced

8 sage leaves, cut into strips

250ml cider

1 tbsp Dijon mustard

1 tbsp honey

sage leaves and flowers, to garnish

TIP Instead of cooking the pork medallions on the stove, you could use a barbecue.

Pigs love apples, sage is great with pork, and apple and sage are a perfect combination. This classic dish works and is exactly what you want to eat in September, when apples are abundant and literally falling off the trees. My father used to serve Valpolicella as an inexpensive substitute for claret. Also, Chianti Classico or any Sangiovese will complement this dish to perfection.

1 Place the pork pieces, one at a time, between two pieces of baking parchment and bash with a rolling pin or meat mallet to make medallions. Season each one with salt and pepper, sprinkle with a little of the oil, then set aside, ready to chargrill at the last minute.

2 Heat the remaining oil in a heavy-based pan over a moderate heat. Cook the red onion until softened, adding a dash of vinegar to retain the bright colour.

3 Add the apples and sage to the pan and fry for 2 minutes. Reduce the heat, stir in the cider, mustard and honey, and season with salt and pepper. Simmer the mixture for 10 minutes to turn it into a compote. Keep warm or set aside to reheat when needed.

4 Place a ribbed griddle pan over a high heat. Sear the pork medallions for 2–3 minutes on each side.

5 Serve on a bed of the apple compote, garnished with extra sage leaves and flowers.

RICHARD'S WINES TO SHARE AND PAIR
The Good Sommelier

We have all seen it: an extravagant gathering at a restaurant, a generous host buying a very special bottle of wine and then a somewhat inebriated guest shouting to the wine waiter: 'Another bottle of the same.'

The experienced sommelier must exercise caution and tact here, before there is upset at the end of the night over an unexpectedly high bill. He insists on representing the fine wine list, flattering the guest's wine expertise by asking him to check his preferred vintage and, at the same time, ensuring he sees the bottle price. If there is a hesitation, the good sommelier quickly makes an alternative, more modest recommendation.

This month I want to recommend a dry, 'salty' manzanilla sherry to accompany the Seashore Soup. I loved the story, by the way. For the Monkfish 'En Croute', I would go for an oaked South African Chenin Blanc; and for the Spatchcocked Chicken, I would recommend a robust Australian Shiraz.

SPATCHCOCKED BARBECUED CHICKEN WITH BRAMBLE & APPLE SALSA

In September the countryside is overflowing with wild blackberries, apples and wild herbs. Alas, you will need to buy the chicken. This simple barbecue recipe is all about cooking and eating out of doors to enjoy the wonderful country we live in.

1 To spatchcock the chicken, turn the bird breast-side down and use a strong pair of kitchen scissors to cut along each side of the backbone, then remove it completely. Now turn the chicken breast-side up and use a heavy fish slice and the palm of your hand to press the bird out flat into a 'butterfly'.

2 Place all the ingredients for the rub in a food processor, reserving a few marjoram leaves for the salsa, and blend until well combined. Rub the mixture into both sides of the chicken and place it in the fridge for a couple of hours, to marinate.

3 Meanwhile, prepare the salsa. Combine all the ingredients in a bowl, including the reserved marjoram leaves, and season to taste with salt and pepper.

4 Cook the chicken on a hot but not flaming barbecue, turning it over several times. It will take only about 20 minutes to cook – but check the densest part to make sure the meat is cooked through.

5 Serve the chicken with the salsa alongside.

SERVES 4–6

a 1.5kg free-range organic chicken

For the rub

100ml rapeseed oil

2 lemons, grated zest and juice

a small bunch of wild marjoram

2 garlic cloves

2 tsp smoked paprika

2 tsp Malvern salt

For the salsa

1 crisp apple, cored and finely diced

100g wild blackberries, halved

1 red onion, diced

a bunch of parsley, chopped

1 tsp chilli flakes

3 tbsp rapeseed oil

1 tbsp red wine vinegar

2 tbsp honey

salt and freshly ground black pepper

PEAR & BLACKBERRY COBBLER

SERVES 6

oil, for greasing

custard or vanilla ice cream, to serve

For the fruit filling

3 conference pears, peeled, cored and cut into chunks

200g blackberries

2 tbsp honey

juice of 1 small lemon

1 tsp ground cinnamon

a pinch of ground cloves (optional)

For the flapjack

200g porridge oats

100g butter

100g brown sugar

3 tbsp golden syrup

2 tsp demerara sugar, for the topping

A cobbler is something between a pie and a crumble – seasonal stewed fruits, with a crunchy crust arranged like cobbles in an ancient street. This recipe uses delicious, juicy conference pears, wild blackberries and flapjack cobbles. We then add a melted brûlée-style topping of demerara sugar. Although there are two stages to this recipe, it is well worth the effort, plus you will get a feast of flapjack offcuts to snack on as a by-product. We haven't said much about dessert wines, but they are always considered a treat and can be the making of a simple pudding. Monbazillac in Bergerac make some cracking sweet wines, or try a South African late-harvest Muscat from Constantia.

1 Preheat the oven to 160°C and line a 24cm x 18cm baking tin with oiled baking paper.

2 For the fruit filling, put the pears and blackberries into a heavy-based pan over a gentle heat. Stir in the honey, lemon juice and spices and simmer the mixture for 4–5 minutes, until the fruit is soft and has made its own juice. Remove the pan from the heat and set aside to cool.

3 For the flapjacks, put the porridge oats, butter, sugar and golden syrup into a heavy-based pan over a moderate heat. Stir with a wooden spoon until the sugar has melted.

4 Turn the mixture on to the baking tin and spread out with a palette knife to form an even layer. Bake the flapjack for 25 minutes, until golden brown. Increase the oven temperature to 180°C.

5 Remove the flapjack from the oven and allow it to cool a little, then, using a 3cm cutter, cut small round cobbles.

6 Put the fruit mix together with all its juice into an ovenproof dish. Arrange the flapjack cobbles evenly on top, then sprinkle with demerara sugar. Bake the cobbler in the oven for 15 minutes.

7 Serve with lashings of custard or vanilla ice cream.

APPLE & PLUM FRANGIPANE SLICE

MAKES 16 SLICES

For the frangipane
100g butter
100g caster sugar
1 egg
100g ground almonds
1 tbsp plain flour
2 tsp vanilla essence

For the slice
200g apples, peeled, cored and sliced
200g plums, quartered and stoned
80g muscovado sugar
40g butter
80ml golden syrup
1 egg
200g plain flour
a pinch of salt

Nutbourne was originally apple orchards. There is an acre or so of the trees remaining. Although now very old, they still provide a glut of fruit in a good season. This recipe is another way of using spare apples, but it is so yummy it would be well worth going out and buying what you need.

1 Make the frangipane. Use an electric hand whisk to blend the butter and sugar together. Keep whisking, add the egg, then the almonds, flour and vanilla essence. Set the mixture aside to use later.

2 Put the apples and plums with the muscovado sugar into a small heavy-based pan over a moderate heat. Bring to the boil, stir, turn off the heat and allow to cool.

3 Again using an electric hand whisk, cream the butter and golden syrup together in a mixing bowl until pale. Add the egg, followed by the flour. When smooth, stir in the fruits and their juices.

4 Transfer the mixture on to the oiled baking tray and dot the frangipane evenly across the top. Bake in a preheated oven at 180°C for 60–75 minutes. Check that the cake is firm in the middle, remove from the oven, leave for 10 minutes, turn out on to a wire rack. Allow to cool completely before cutting into even slices.

A BIRD'S EYE VIEW

*An artist can somehow provide an aerial view of the landscape without
the aid of drone cameras.*

*Bridget clearly sees the vineyard like a bird from high above: the structural end posts
supporting row upon row of vines leading into the distance, where a line of trees is
breaking the wind coming over the hill. The natural colours merge but the man-made trellis
stands out stark in blue, acknowledging our impact on the land.*

October

The grape harvest is underway but alongside the main event are quinces, damsons, aubergines, pumpkins and Cox's apples. The bounty of autumn – ripe and resplendent.

THIS MONTH'S FOOD CHAMPIONS	SOURCE	CHARACTER & COMMENT	RECIPES
salad leaves	markets, good greengrocers or grow your own	varied, textured, fresh, healthy	October Salad
pumpkin	farm shops, markets, good greengrocers	wholesome, honey, fibrous	Pumpkin Scones
aubergine	good greengrocers or grow your own	mild, tender, a carrier of other flavours	Stuffed Aubergine
wild chervil	foraged from woodlands, parks and gardens	delicate, liquorice, grassy	Red Gurnard, Pumpkin Scones
red gurnard	good fishmongers, sourced from UK	mild, flaky, meaty, succulent	Red Gurnard
venison	game dealers, good butchers	lean, tender, rich	Braised Venison
quince	orchards, good greengrocers	lemony, pears, perfumed, granular	Treacle & Quince Tart
damsons and sloes	forage in hedgerows	intense, plum, zesty, lasting	Chocolate Truffles, Pumpkin Scones
chestnuts	trees, farmers' markets, good greengrocers	buttery, sweet, nutty, fulfilling	Sausage Rolls, Braised Venison
rosehips	forage in hedgerows or on wild seashores	fruity, tangy, sweet	Rosehip Chutney

PUMPKIN SCONES, WHIPPED GOAT'S CHEESE & DAMSONS

MAKES 12

150g pumpkin flesh

2 tbsp pumpkin seeds

a knob of butter

225g self-raising flour

½ tsp salt

150g Cheddar cheese, grated

freshly ground black pepper

150ml milk

1 egg

For the topping

200g damsons

50g caster sugar

1 tbsp balsamic vinegar

150g goat's cheese

2 tbsp natural yoghurt

a few sprigs of wild chervil

It is important to know your own limitations – and my pastry skills are certainly limited. Years ago I used to do large-scale cookery demonstrations as charity fundraisers – they were light-hearted and fun. On one particular occasion we had an audience of over 300, with a full-scale stage and monitors set under spotlights. I was attempting to make a pastry case and the pastry literally melted in my hot hands. This created great hilarity with the audience. My assistant, an extremely talented chef named Olivia Stewart Cox, whispered in my ear, could she have a go? With delicate, fast-moving fingers, cool as a cucumber, she immediately recovered the dough and in a matter of seconds made a perfect pastry case. This brought the house down; it was so well choreographed that most of the audience assumed we had staged the whole thing deliberately! So now I avoid pastry but, luckily, Bridget too has the magic touch. The secret to making scones is to be quick, a bit rough and ready, and don't overwork the dough.

1 Grate the pumpkin on a coarse cheese-grater. Heat a knob of butter in a small pan over a moderate heat. Cook the grated pumpkin for 2–3 minutes, to soften, toss in the pumpkin seeds, set aside to cool.

2 Sift the flour and salt into a mixing bowl. Add the grated cheese and fried pumpkin, rub together with your fingertips to the consistency of breadcrumbs. Season the mixture with black pepper, make a well in the centre, pour in the milk, then the egg, and quickly bring the mixture together with your fingers.

3 Turn the dough out on to a floured surface, knead it lightly, then roll it out to an even 3cm thickness. Using a 6cm pastry cutter, stamp out 12 rounds, re-rolling the dough as necessary.

4 Place the scones on the baking tin lined with baking paper, brush the tops with a little milk, cook in a preheated oven at 190°C for 12 minutes.

5 Now prepare the toppings. Cook the damsons, sugar and vinegar over a moderate heat until soft, then fish out the stones with a slotted spoon. Whip the goat's cheese with an electric hand whisk, add the yoghurt a little at a time until you get a nice consistency.

6 Halve the scones, spread with a generous dollop of goat's cheese, top each one with the cooked damsons and decorate with wild chervil.

OCTOBER SALAD: LAST OF THE SUMMER LEAVES & BEETROOT FALAFEL

Although we are into October, there are still some lovely salad leaves in the greenhouse and the vegetable garden or available at farmers' markets. Red oak-leaf, mizuna and lamb's tongue all have a lovely flavour and, together with a variety of green herbs, give us a chance to extend the salad-eating season. We also have an autumn crop of sweet, tangy beetroots to make these delightful baked falafel. They are a lovely explosion of flavour to contrast with the gentle leaves. I would drink a Semillon-Sauvignon blend or white Viognier from the southern hemisphere to contrast with this home-grown salad.

1 Begin by preparing the falafel. Place the beetroot, onion, garlic, chickpeas and the herbs, including the stalks, in a food processor and blitz them until well combined.

2 Add the spices, salt and baking powder, then blitz again. Rest the mixture in the fridge for 1 hour.

3 Preheat the oven to 200°C. Line a baking tray with baking paper. Mix the onion seeds with the rapeseed oil on a shallow plate. Using your hands, form the falafel mixture into 2–3cm balls, squash them into patties, then coat them with the oiled seeds.

4 Place the patties on the baking tray lined with baking paper, place in the oven and cook for 6 minutes on one side, flip them over and cook for a further 4 minutes.

5 To serve, arrange the salad leaves and herbs in a salad bowl. Drizzle with oil and lemon juice, sprinkle with rock salt, then scatter the hot, freshly baked falafel on top. Serve right away.

SERVES 4–6

3 or 4 types of salad leaves

green herbs: chicory tops, chervil, basil and mint

virgin rapeseed oil

lemon juice

rock salt flakes

For the falafel

3 medium-sized raw beetroots, washed and grated

1 red onion, roughly chopped

1 garlic clove, sliced

400g can of chickpeas, rinsed and drained

a small bunch of parsley

a small bunch of mint

2 tsp ground cumin

2 tsp ground coriander

1 tsp chilli flakes

1 tsp sea salt

a pinch of baking powder

1 tbsp black onion seeds

1 tbsp rapeseed oil

TIP Instead of cooking the falafel in an oven, you could use an air fryer. There is no need to use a baking tray: place them directly on to the grid.

HARVEST SAUSAGE ROLLS

MAKES 24

1 tbsp rapeseed oil

1 red onion, finely sliced

60g sultanas

60g chestnuts, fully peeled

1 tbsp red wine vinegar

400g minced pork

3 sage leaves, shredded

½ tsp ground nutmeg

salt and freshly ground black pepper

320g sheet of ready-rolled puff pastry

a little flour

1 free-range egg

a little milk

2 tsp nigella seeds

The whole family gets involved in the harvest, plus a large, local team of enthusiasts. They pick the grapes by hand: it is a lot of hard, back-aching work, so a bit of motivational nourishment never goes amiss. These 'best ever' sausage rolls do just what they are supposed to. Whether you are picking vast quantities of wine grapes, painting the garage door or weeding the allotment, they are just the ticket.

1 Put the oil into a small heavy-based pan over a moderate heat. Fry the onion for 2 minutes, stir in the sultanas, chestnuts and vinegar (the vinegar preserves the red onion's colour), cook for a further 4 minutes, until soft.

2 Put the minced pork into a mixing bowl, add the cooked onion mixture, sage and nutmeg, season with salt and pepper, blend the mixture together with a wooden spoon or gloved hands.

3 Sprinkle flour on the work surface and place the puff pastry sheet on to it. Cut the sheet lengthways into three. Divide the pork mixture into three and place the meat evenly along the strips of pastry.

4 Mix the egg with a little milk and a pinch of salt. Roll the pastry over the meat filling, use the egg mix to seal the join. Brush the top of the pastry rolls with the remaining egg mix.

5 Cut each length into 8 even-sized pieces. Sprinkle the tops with nigella seeds, transfer to a baking sheet lined with baking paper and bake in a preheated oven at 200°C for 20 minutes, until golden.

6 Allow to cool a little before serving, or chill and reheat when required.

COX'S APPLE & ROSEHIP CHUTNEY

This chutney is a great accompaniment to our Harvest Sausage Rolls, or serve it with any mature hard cheese. All rosehips are edible, but dog rosehip (often found growing wild along a pebbly seashore), has an especially lovely tangy flavour, which complements the Cox's apples well.

MAKES 2 X 450ML JARS

150g rosehips, cut in half

200ml cider vinegar

400g Cox's apples, peeled, cored and cut into chunks

1 onion, chopped

150g muscovado sugar

2 tsp mustard seeds

2 tsp ground mixed spice

½ tsp salt

1 Put the rosehips and cider vinegar into a large pan over a gentle heat. Bring to the boil, then reduce the heat and simmer for 15 minutes.

2 Add all the other ingredients to the pan and continue to cook until the onions are soft.

3 Remove the pan from the heat, allow the chutney to cool, then transfer to sterilized jars.

TIP The chutney will mature with age like a fine wine. Store it in a cool place but, once opened, keep it in the fridge and use within a couple of weeks.

OLIVER'S TALES FROM A FORAGER'S DIARY
What Grows Together Goes Together

I walk through the countryside with my eyes scanning the earth and vegetation, hoping to see some delicious natural ingredient that I recognize or, better still, something I don't. It is the possibility of discovering an edible something for the first time that builds the excitement and draws me into the undergrowth.

As both a forager and a chef I create recipes with a simple ethos: 'What grows together goes together.' Today I have found meadowsweet along the damp edge of a stream. The roe deer browse here on wild berries and meadowsweet. I therefore serve a dish of venison with meadowsweet and wild berry jam.

The same goes for so many other natural pairings: rabbit with young nettles, grouse with heather flowers, or hake with sea purlane. Nature does the work for us, marrying great flavours together that we can observe in the wild and then bring back together in the kitchen.

STUFFED AUBERGINE, CAULIFLOWER, RAISIN & ALMOND

SERVES 4

4 Black Beauty aubergines (or similar)

½ white cauliflower, cored and diced

½ purple cauliflower, cored and cut into small florets

1 green apple, peeled, cored and diced

60g raisins

60g almond nibs

2 tbsp rapeseed oil

60ml plain yoghurt

salt and freshly ground black pepper

½ tsp sumac

nasturtium petals

I have a godson named Philip who runs the most marvellous pub in the Cotswolds: The Bull, in Charlbury. Part of his success is that he too grows his own vegetables, salads and fruits. So, after having a wonderful overindulgent lunch in the pub, we went to visit Philip's nearby smallholding. It was a feast for the eyes as well as the plate: a paradise of abundant produce both outdoors and inside a polytunnel. There were a few free-range chickens scratching around among it all. How the chickens don't spoil the crops I don't know – but there was so much growing that perhaps a little sharing is not an issue. We inspected row upon row of bright fresh lettuces and vegetables. We saw every kind of bean, kale, brassicas, neat little beds of herbs, high trellises of cucumbers and tomatoes, every kind of cauliflower, peppers and more. Best of all were these perfect aubergines hanging generously on their bushes. Like the chickens, I was invited to help myself to a few and, when we got home, we stuffed them for supper with two colours of cauliflower, plus apple, raisins and almond nibs.

1 Preheat the oven to 200°C. Halve the aubergines lengthways and carefully cut out the flesh, leaving the outside 'shell' intact.

2 Dice the aubergine flesh. Reserve a little of the cauliflower, apple, raisins and almonds, add the remainder to the diced aubergine, mix to combine, then season with salt and pepper.

3 Whisk the oil into the yoghurt, season with sumac, salt and pepper, then spread this mixture inside the aubergine shells. Place the aubergines on a baking tray and fill with the diced vegetable mixture, cover with foil, then cook in the oven for 20 minutes.

4 Before serving, decorate the stuffed aubergine with a few extra pieces of raw cauliflower, apple and raisins, then finish with nasturtium petals.

RED GURNARD WITH BUTTERNUT RISOTTO

Red gurnard is an often underrated fish but its mild, delicate, sweet flesh makes for great eating, especially when served with a vegetable-based risotto. There are three elements to this recipe: the tomato concasse, which can be prepared well in advance; the fish, which virtually cooks itself; the risotto, best cooked just before serving, which you can concentrate on. Our own Nutbourne Barrel Reserve would be a good pairing for this dish, but so would a robust Chenin Blanc or Chardonnay from South Africa or Chile.

SERVES 4

800g red gurnard, cleaned, descaled and cut into 4 portions

oil

salt and freshly ground black pepper

For the concasse

300g multicoloured heritage tomatoes, deseeded and diced

2–3 tbsp parsley, chopped

1 tbsp rapeseed oil

For the risotto

1 butternut squash, peeled, cored and cut into 2–3cm cubes

150ml white wine

1 lemon, grated zest and juice

2 tbsp sunflower oil

1 white onion

1 garlic clove

250g arborio rice

wild chervil, to serve

1 Preheat the oven to 200°C. Oil and season the gurnard fillets, then place them in an ovenproof dish, ready to bake.

2 Prepare the concasse. Put the diced tomatoes and parsley into a small bowl, add the oil, then season with salt and pepper. Leave at room temperature to develop flavour.

3 Next, prepare a butternut purée as the base for the risotto. Bring a pan of lightly-salted water to the boil over a moderate heat, add the butternut, cook for 15 minutes, then drain, reserving the cooking liquid.

4 Transfer the butternut to a blender and blitz to a purée. You may need to add a little of the cooking liquid. Transfer the purée to a measuring jug and add the white wine, lemon zest and juice and more of the vegetable cooking water to make up to 750ml.

5 Heat the sunflower oil in a heavy-based pan over a moderate heat. Fry the onion and garlic until soft, stir in the rice, season, then cook the rice and onion together for 2 minutes, stirring, until the rice becomes opaque.

6 Now start to add the butternut cooking liquid, a little at a time, as it is absorbed into the rice. Stop cooking when the rice has swelled but still has a little bite to it. This will take approximately 15 minutes.

7 While the risotto is cooking, bake the gurnard in the oven for 8 minutes. The flesh should be pearly but not raw.

8 Present the risotto in the pan with the red gurnard fillets placed on top and the concasse spooned over. Finish with wild chervil.

BRAISED VENISON WITH GRAPES, CHESTNUTS & RED WINE

SERVES 6

50g butter

2 red onions, chopped

2 garlic cloves, crushed

1kg venison haunch, trimmed and cubed

50g plain flour

salt and freshly ground black pepper

400ml red wine

400ml chicken stock (a stock cube dissolved in hot water is fine)

1 tbsp Dijon mustard

2 tbsp redcurrant or cranberry jelly

8 sage leaves, shredded

1 tbsp red wine vinegar

150g cooked chestnuts, roughly chopped

200g black grapes, quartered

chicory tops, to finish

As the days draw in and autumn becomes a reality, we begin to yearn for some comfort food. This is a lovely, wholesome casserole with which we celebrate the end of the grape harvest. There are now some wonderful Pinot Noir wines grown in unexpected parts of the world including Germany, Italy, New Zealand, Oregon and even England – this dish cries out for one.

1 Heat the butter in a solid casserole dish over a moderate heat, add the onion and garlic, fry until soft.

2 Coat the venison meat in seasoned flour, add the meat to the casserole, fry it for about 2 minutes, until evenly browned.

3 Stir in the wine, stock, mustard, jelly, sage, vinegar, salt and pepper.

4 Bring to the boil, then reduce the heat, place a lid on the casserole and gently simmer for 1½ hours, stirring occasionally.

5 After this time, taste the sauce, adjust the seasoning and check that the meat is melt-in-the-mouth tender.

6 When ready to serve, stir in the chestnuts, sprinkle over the grapes and finish with chicory leaves.

SHOREHAM-BY-SEA

*Bridget painted these huge canvasses on the shoreline at Shoreham-by-Sea – a jumble
of industrial structure and high activity on the island docks. Throughout the summer months,
these paintings are displayed on the outside wall of our buildings as a welcome to visitors
and as an introduction to the workings of the winery inside.*

RICHARD'S WINES TO SHARE AND PAIR
Four Harvests in One Year

My one claim to fame in the wine world is that I once managed to take part in four different grape harvests in a single calendar year. The first was in Marlborough, South Island, NZ, where I worked the night shift, seven days per week, non-stop for two months, processing Sauvignon Blanc. From there I went to a specialist Cabernet Sauvignon producer called Abreu Vineyards in Napa Valley, where the crop was picked in early August. Along with a team of 30 Mexican workers, I hand-selected, berry by berry, to choose only the very best. We processed a single ton of fruit per day to make a very exclusive wine. In September I flew back from America to join the team at Champagne Lagache: they are great family friends who really do start a vendange day with a crisp glass of their own product at 5am – a treat I have sadly had to grow out of. Then finally back home to England for our own harvest at Nutbourne throughout October.

My choices in October are to serve a zingy New Zealand Sauvignon with the Stuffed Aubergine, a rich Californian Cabernet Sauvignon with the Braised Venison, Nutbourne Pinot Noir with the Sausage Rolls, and an irresistible glass of Lagache Champagne at every possible opportunity.

OLIVIA'S SLOE GIN CHOCOLATE TRUFFLES

Olivia Thomas manages our sales, hospitality and visitor experience at the vineyard. She is an indispensable member of the team. Many assume she is part of the family and she might as well be: her enthusiasm and contribution are second to none. She is also a forager and a bit of a quirky cook, so when she told me about Sloe Gin Chocolate Truffles I instantly gave them a place in this book. This is also an opportunity to provide a recipe for the sloe gin. Sloes are a type of wild plum found in the hedgerows in many areas of Britain. The little fruits are too tart and tannic to eat fresh but they make a wonderful liqueur with its own distinct flavour. Like a fine wine, sloe gin develops over time, so I recommend you make enough this year for next year's batch of chocolate truffles – they will taste even better.

MAKES 24

For the sloe gin
400g sloes
1 cinnamon stick
200g golden caster sugar
70cl gin

For the truffles
300g 70% dark chocolate
150ml double cream
60g butter
40ml sloe gin
2 heaped tbsp cocoa powder

1 To make the sloe gin, first wash the freshly picked sloes, then spread them out on a tea towel to dry. Prick them individually with a sharp fork, then pack them into a large Kilner jar.

2 Add the cinnamon, sugar and gin to the jar. (Any brand will do – you really don't need a special one.)

3 Seal the jar, shake well, then place somewhere away from the sunlight. Shake the jar daily for the next 7–10 days, then set aside to mature for two months.

4 When you are fed up with waiting, filter and bottle the sloe gin. To do this, line a sieve with muslin cloth, place this over a jug and carefully pour the mixture through it. Allow time for the liquid to thoroughly drain, then discard the sloes and cinnamon. If needed, filter the liquid for a second time: it should be crystal clear. Decant it into small glass bottles, seal and leave to mature. The liqueur will last for many years.

5 To make the chocolate truffles, grate the chocolate into a glass bowl. Heat the cream, butter and sloe gin together in a small pan over a gentle heat and bring to simmering point.

6 Pour the cream mixture over the chocolate and stir together until smooth. Transfer to the fridge for 2 hours, to set.

7 Sift the cocoa powder on to a plate. Using a melon baller, scoop even rounds from the truffle mixture. Chill your hands under the cold tap, dry them well, then roll the chocolate balls in your palms. Lay the balls on to the cocoa and roll them gently, to evenly coat the outside.

8 Chill the finished truffles in the fridge before serving or packaging them up as presents.

TREACLE & QUINCE TART

SERVES 8–10

For the pastry case

150g plain flour, plus extra for dusting

40g icing sugar

a pinch of salt

75g butter, diced, plus extra for greasing

1 large egg, lightly beaten

1 tbsp lemon juice

For the quince filling

400g quince, cored, peeled and diced

3 tbsp honey

50g butter

½ tsp ground nutmeg

2 egg yolks

For the treacle filling

200ml golden syrup

100g fresh breadcrumbs

1 lemon, zest and juice

2 tbsp double cream

This is a great autumnal pudding – a sweet pastry tart case with a layer of enriched quince purée and then a layer of treacle. Serve this with a dollop of crème fraiche or whipped cream and accompany it with small shots of chilled Pedro Ximénez, an incredibly sweet, treacly dark sherry that tastes fantastic.

---

1 To make the pastry, mix the flour, sugar and salt together in a large bowl. Use your fingertips to rub the diced butter into the mixture to form 'breadcrumbs'. Make a well in the flour, pour in the egg and lemon juice, then knead gently to form a smooth dough.

2 Wrap the pastry in cling film and chill in the fridge for at least an hour.

3 Preheat the oven to 200°C. Grease a deep 18cm tart tin with a little butter. Sprinkle some flour on to the work surface and roll out the pastry to an even circle, a bit bigger than the tin.

4 Fit the pastry into the tin and neatly trim off any excess. Prick the base of the pastry case with a fork, crumple a piece of baking paper, fit this inside the pastry case and fill with baking beans or uncooked rice.

5 Place the pastry case in the oven and bake blind for 10 minutes. Remove the baking beans and paper and return the case to the oven for a further 10 minutes. Remove from the oven and reduce the heat to 180°C.

6 Prepare the quince purée. Put the quince, honey and butter into a heavy-based pan over a low heat, add 3 tbsp of water and cook for 20 minutes, until the fruit is soft.

7 Transfer the quince to a food processor and blitz to a purée; add the nutmeg and egg yolks, blitz again, then set aside.

8 When the pastry case is cooked, spread the quince purée across the base.

9 For the treacle filling, melt the syrup in a heavy-based pan, add the breadcrumbs, the lemon zest and juice and the cream. Bring to the boil, stirring, then pour this mixture over the quince to completely fill the tart case.

10 Place the tart in the oven and bake for 30 minutes. Serve warm.

November

Warm coats and wellies are needed for intrepid foraging walks. We are on the lookout for woodland mushrooms, wild nuts, game birds, fallow deer and medlars.

THIS MONTH'S FOOD CHAMPIONS	SOURCE	CHARACTER & COMMENT	RECIPES
hazelnuts	farmers' markets and good stores – buy British	crunch, earthy, satisfying	Mushroom Soufflé
medlars	forage, and pick your own	intense, exotic	Medlar Jelly
young root vegetables	markets and good greengrocers	tender, earthy, wholesome	November Salad
wild mushrooms	foraging the last of the season	perfumed, aromatic, lasting	Mushroom Soufflé
pheasant and partridge	shoots, game dealers and good butchers	lean, succulent, tender	November Salad, Partridge Saltimbocca
brown shrimps	good fishmongers	like lobster, sweet, flavourful	Pollock En Papillote
fallow deer	game dealers	lean, dark, wild	Fallow Deer Loin
seeds – pumpkin, sunflower, poppy	all food stores	nutritious, crunchy, varied	Leek Hearts, Fallow Deer Loin
hispi cabbage	markets, good greengrocers	tender, herby	Fallow Deer Loin
cooking apples	good greengrocers	sharp, creamy, lasting	Mincemeat & Baked Apples

MEDLAR JELLY

MAKES 4 X 420G JARS

2kg medlars

3 lemons, thickly sliced

2l water

800g caster sugar
(approximate weight)

This might seem a rather obscure recipe to include, but if you can find a couple of kilos of medlars in a farmers' market or, better still, a tree laden with the fruit, you will not be disappointed. Medlars are picked late in the autumn, but ripened off the tree. The jelly has a lovely, deep flavour and exotic, amber-red colour. We serve it with partridge, duck, soft cheeses or just on buttered crumpets. It is truly delicious. To achieve a good jelly, you need both soft, ripe medlars and some firm, underripe ones to give sufficient pectin for setting. We achieve this by picking the crop when the fruit is just beginning to soften, then storing about a quarter of them in the fridge to prevent further ripening. The remaining fruit is placed on a tray in a single layer, stored in a dark place at room temperature for about 10 days, after which time they will have softened and turned dark brown. The old-fashioned term for this is 'bletting' the medlars.

1 Check the medlars for any rot and remove these patches. Cut both the ripe medlars and the hard ones (from the fridge) into halves, discarding any leaves or stems.

2 Put the medlars and lemons in a large saucepan, add the water and bring to the boil over a moderate heat.

3 Reduce the heat to a gentle simmer, place a lid on the pan and cook for 1 hour, then allow to cool.

4 Line a large bowl or jug with muslin cloth. Transfer the fruit and liquid into the cloth and tie it with a string.

5 Now you need to suspend the cloth above the bowl so the liquid can gently drip through. You might have to rig something up for this, or hang the bag from a kitchen mixer tap.

6 Leave it to drip for a few hours, then squeeze the muslin bag to extract as much juice as you can, leaving a relatively dry pulp, which can be discarded.

7 Measure the volume of medlar liquid, then measure out the same weight of caster sugar. Place the two in a saucepan over a high heat, bring to the boil and cook rapidly for 5 minutes.

8 Allow the jelly to cool a little, then decant it into sterilized jars. Seal and store for up to 2 years. (We actually have some jellies dating back 10 years that are still very edible, but food safety prevents me from recommending that.)

OLIVER'S TALES FROM A FORAGER'S DIARY
The Naming of a Restaurant

It is early morning in late November. The mist is clearing to give bright dappled shafts of sunshine through the damp woodland canopy. The ground is soft and fertile, layered with millennia of vegetation. Here in the undisturbed countryside lies a treasure trove of wild animals, herbs and fungi just waiting for the enthusiastic forager to harvest for the cooking pot.

Pigeons and rabbits are woodland favourites, although jay birds and squirrels are good options when it comes to walking with a gun.

My brother, Richard, and I were out hunting but also discussing what we should call our new restaurant venture. Suddenly, up ahead in a clearing I spotted a rabbit. I am a decent shot, got the rabbit, collected it and waved it in the air, shouting, 'This is true local and wild food.'

We knew there and then that the restaurant's name would be RABBIT, Chelsea. Now, 10 years on, it continues to thrive, celebrating all things the countryside has on offer.

WILD MUSHROOM & HAZELNUT CHEESE SOUFFLÉ

Why do we so rarely cook soufflés? They are relatively quick to rustle up, infinitely variable, utterly delicious and, if you follow the recipe correctly, a culinary triumph! We have made this seasonal soufflé with wild mushrooms, hazelnuts and mature Cheddar cheese. It can be served as a starter or a main course. We need a few wine recommendations to go with this. Chinon in the Loire Valley make lovely delicate Cabernet Franc, well worth a try. Or, at the other end of the scale (and budget), a fine premier cru Chablis with all its subtlety and fineness.

SERVES 4–6

200g wild mushrooms, diced

80g hazelnuts, chopped

a little cooking oil

30g butter, plus extra for greasing

30g plain flour

150ml milk

salt and freshly ground black pepper

cayenne pepper

1 tbsp Dijon mustard

150g Cheddar cheese, grated

6 large eggs, separated

1 Begin by preparing a 1-litre soufflé dish: butter the inside, then fold and tie a sheet of greaseproof paper around the outside. This enables the soufflé to rise out of the dish without toppling over the sides.

2 Place a heavy-based pan over a moderate heat, add a little oil and fry the mushrooms and hazelnuts.

3 Remove the mixture from the pan and drain on kitchen paper to absorb the juices; allow to cool.

4 In the same pan, melt the butter, stir in the flour, then cook and stir for 2 minutes to make a roux. Slowly add the milk, a little at a time, while continuing to stir, season with salt, pepper, a pinch of cayenne and Dijon mustard.

5 Remove the pan from the heat and stir in the grated cheese and the mushroom mix.

6 When you can hold your hand against the warm side of the pan, stir in the egg yolks.

7 Place the egg whites in a clean, dry mixing bowl and, using an electric beater, whisk into stiff peaks. (This means the whites should be firm and dry, holding their shape.)

8 Fold half the stiff whites into the mixture in the pan, then fold in the second half, keeping the mixture as light and airy as possible. Gently spoon the soufflé mixture into the prepared dish.

9 At this stage the soufflé can be kept in the fridge for up to 2 hours before baking.

10 When you are ready to cook, preheat the oven to 200°C, then bake the soufflé for 30–35 minutes. It will rise out of the dish and be golden brown on top.

11 Remove the paper collar and serve immediately to great applause.

LEEK HEARTS, SOUR CREAM, SUNFLOWER SEEDS & TRUFFLE

SERVES 4-6

4 leeks, cut into varied 5–8cm lengths

100ml sour cream

1 tbsp honey

1 garlic clove, chopped

2 tsp sherry vinegar

60ml rapeseed oil

salt and pepper

50g sunflower seeds, roasted

For the garnish

nasturtium leaves

marigold petals

chive flowers

green herb oil

1 fresh black truffle

Leeks grow plentifully in our veg garden and we need to be quite inventive not to get tired of them. This is a lovely way to prepare and serve leeks as an unusual starter.

1 Put a flat griddle plate over a high heat until very hot. Sear the leeks on all sides to blacken the outsides and tenderize the hearts inside.

2 Strip off the black outer leaves, set the hearts aside to cool. Put the blackened leaves in a hot oven (or air fryer) for a few minutes to dry out, then blitz them in a blender to make leek ash.

3 Put the sour cream, honey, garlic and vinegar into a blender. With the blade running, slowly pour in the oil to form an emulsion; season with salt and pepper.

4 Spread the sunflower seeds on to a baking sheet, toast in the oven for 6 minutes (or use an air fryer).

5 To assemble the dish, gently warm the leek hearts. Spoon the sour cream dressing on the base of a serving plate, arrange the leeks on top, and finish with seeds, nasturtium leaves, marigold petals, leek ash and, at the last minute, shavings of black truffle.

NOVEMBER SALAD: ROOT VEGETABLES WITH PHEASANT, COMICE PEAR & WALNUTS

Generally, the salads in this book have been about using the best vegetables of the season, and this one is no exception: young parsnips, sweet potatoes and baby turnips, together with comice pear and toasted walnuts. But I wanted a salad that also uses the spare meat of game.

1 Preheat the oven to 190°C. Put the onion, parsnips, sweet potato and turnips together in a roasting tin. Toss in sunflower oil and thyme and season with salt and pepper. Place in the oven and roast for 30 minutes.

2 Meanwhile, make the marinade. In a small bowl, mix together the molasses, mustard, vinegar and walnut oil, then season to taste with salt and pepper. Coat the cooked pheasant meat in this mixture and leave for an hour, to marinate.

3 Heat a small heavy-based frying pan over a gentle heat. Toss in the walnuts and cook, stirring occasionally, for 2 minutes, then add the pheasant and marinade to the pan, bring to the boil and heat through for a couple of minutes.

4 Transfer the roasted vegetables to a serving dish. Arrange the raw pear slices on top, spoon over the hot pheasant together with all the juices, scatter with chives and serve warm.

SERVES 4–6

1 red onion, sliced

2 parsnips, peeled and cut into sticks

1 sweet potato, peeled and cubed

3 baby turnips, cut into wedges

2 tbsp sunflower oil

a few sprigs of wild thyme

salt and freshly ground black pepper

300–400g cooked pheasant meat, cut into strips

50g walnuts, shelled

1 comice pear, cored and sliced into half-moons

chives, to garnish

For the marinade

2 tbsp pomegranate molasses

1 tbsp Dijon mustard

1 tbsp sherry vinegar

2 tbsp walnut oil

FALLOW DEER LOIN, HISPI RED CABBAGE, HONEY, SEED & MINT GASTRIQUE

Fallow deer is wonderful, tender, lean wild meat. There are apparently more wild deer in the UK these days than there have been for the past 1,000 years. All the natural predators such as wolves, bears and lynx have become extinct and hunting today is strictly limited. So if you get the chance to cook and enjoy these lovely wild pests, go for it: you will be doing the countryside a favour. Hispi cabbage, sometimes called pointy cabbage or sweetheart cabbage, has always been around, but it has now become fashionable. As for gastrique, this is a classic preparation of sweet and sour, using caramelized sugar combined with vinegar and, in this case, lots of different seeds. I think it complements the deer beautifully.

SERVES 4

800g loin of fallow deer, trimmed and tied

1 red hispi cabbage, cut into quarters and cored

3 tbsp sunflower oil

For the marinade

1 sprig of rosemary, stems removed

2 tsp coriander seeds

1 garlic clove, crushed

40ml rapeseed oil

salt and freshly ground black pepper

For the honey gastrique

4 tbsp honey

½ red onion, finely chopped

40g sunflower seeds

40g poppy seeds

40g pumpkin seeds

4 tbsp white wine vinegar

sprigs of lemon mint, shredded

1 Put the deer in an ovenproof dish. Combine all the marinade ingredients and rub this mixture over the meat; leave in the fridge overnight.

2 To make the gastrique, put the honey in a small pan over a moderate heat, bring to the boil, then reduce the heat and simmer for 2 minutes, to caramelize.

3 Add the onion and seeds to the pan and stir in the vinegar: take care, as the liquid will sizzle. Season with salt and pepper, bring back up to heat, then reduce the heat and simmer until it has reduced by a third. Put aside until ready to serve.

4 Preheat the oven to 200°C. Place a cast-iron griddle plate over a high heat. When it is smoky hot, lift the deer loin out of the marinade and sear the meat on all sides. Return it to the marinade, ready to roast in the oven.

5 Keep the griddle very hot. Spoon the sunflower oil over the cabbage and rub it in. Now sear the cabbage pieces on the griddle, turning occasionally to char on all sides, then transfer to a roasting tin, ready to finish off in the oven.

6 Roast the deer in the marinade in the oven for 8–10 minutes. Remove it from the oven and allow to rest for 10 minutes.

7 While the meat is resting, pop the cabbage into the oven to cook through for 5 minutes; reheat the gastrique on the hob at the same time.

8 To serve, carve the roe deer across the grain and arrange on individual plates with the charred hispi. Stir shredded lemon mint into the gastrique and serve alongside. Garnish with extra lemon mint.

185

PARTRIDGE SALTIMBOCCA

SERVES 4

4 partridge breasts
(or 8 if you are greedy)

4 sage leaves

4 thin slices of lemon

4 slices of Parma ham

salt and freshly ground black pepper

40g unsalted butter

30ml red wine

1 tsp balsamic vinegar

1 tsp honey

1 tsp French mustard

80g red grapes,
halved and seeded

salad leaves, to serve

Richard and Oliver first opened The Shed restaurant in 2012 and it has been a huge success ever since. One of their early traditions was to offer the well-heeled, local residents of Notting Hill 'Beers for Birds'. Early in the week, after a weekend away shooting, regular customers would bring in a few brace of partridge, pheasant or grouse, donate them to The Shed kitchen and, in exchange, have some complimentary drinks in the bar. They would, of course, then be tempted to stay for dinner and make an evening of it – a win-win for all concerned.

1 Carefully cut a pocket into the middle of each partridge breast without splitting it into two pieces. Put a sage leaf and a slice of lemon inside each, wrap a slice of ham tightly around and season with salt and pepper.

2 Place a heavy-based frying pan over a moderate heat, melt the butter in the pan. Fry the breasts for 2–3 minutes on each side, remove from the pan and keep warm.

3 Return the frying pan to a high heat, add the wine, balsamic, honey and mustard. Let it sizzle capturing all the pan flavours, stir rapidly, then toss in the grapes.

4 Carve each partridge breast into 3 pieces and arrange on a bed of salad leaves. Spoon over the glaze and grapes, serve immediately.

POLLOCK EN PAPILLOTE

When Oliver showed us this dish, it was an instant winner. Pollock fillets with brown shrimps on a bed of curly kale, steamed in their own juices: so simple and yet capturing huge flavour, plus the visual delight of each guest opening an individual package. Oliver, of course, cooked his parcels in the outdoor vinewood oven, which gives a mild smoky dimension to the dish – but that is not strictly necessary if you are making it at home. I recommend a wine pairing of bone-dry fermented New World Riesling from Australia, New Zealand or the USA.

SERVES 4

250g curly kale, washed and broken into pieces

4 pollock fillets, each 150g

80g brown shrimps

1 tbsp capers

1 red chilli, thinly sliced

a few parsley sprigs

juice of 2 lemons

salt and freshly ground black pepper

1 Preheat the oven to 200°C. Cut four 25cm rounds of baking paper; crumple each one into a ball, then spread it out again.

2 Make a bed of kale in the middle of each circle, place a piece of pollock on top, then scatter over the shrimps, capers, chilli and parsley. Squeeze lemon juice over each one and season with salt and pepper.

3 Gather the edges of the paper together to form a 'moneybag' parcel. Bind the top of each parcel with cotton thread. Transfer to a roasting tin.

4 Bake the papillotes in the oven for 12 minutes, then remove from the oven and allow them to sit for 5 more minutes before serving.

5 We recommend that you invite your guests to open their own parcels at the table: the initial steamy aroma is amazing.

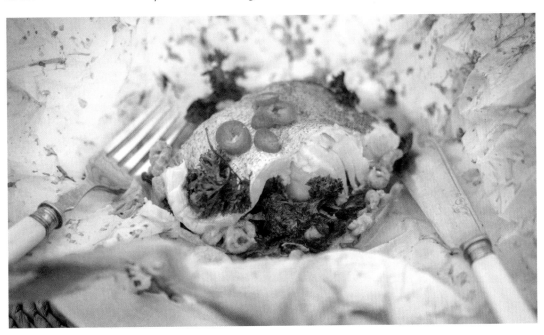

GRANDMOTHER'S MINCEMEAT & BAKED APPLES

For the mincemeat

MAKES 4 X 500G JARS

1kg Bramley cooking apples, cored, peeled and diced

400g suet, beef or vegetarian

400g raisins

400g currants

100g mixed peel

2 lemons, diced rind and juice

2 oranges, diced rind and juice

2 tsp ground mixed spice

1 tsp salt

600g dark soft brown sugar

100ml brandy

100ml dark rum

For the baked apples

SERVES 4

4 medium-sized Bramley cooking apples

240g Grandmother's Mincemeat

40g butter

soft brown sugar

We are not talking about Granny Bridget here! She has an old family hardback notebook with handwritten recipes carefully inscribed by her mother and maybe even her mother's mother! I am a believer that there is no such thing as pure innovation in cooking: all new ideas and recipes are an evolution from something that has been done before. But there are also some ideas that don't need reinventing at all: homemade mincemeat with a baked apple is one of them.

1 Put all the ingredients for the mincemeat together in a large mixing bowl, stir with a wooden spoon until well combined, then allow to infuse for an hour. Stir and leave twice more before bottling.

2 Sterilize the jars by putting them through the dishwasher. Fill the jars, tightly packing the mincemeat down until there is a little liquid at the top. Seal the jars and store in a cool place.

3 Now for the baked apples. Use an old-fashioned coring knife to make a cylindrical hole through the middle of each apple, then use a paring knife to score a line around the circumference of each one.

4 Place the apples in an ovenproof dish, fill the central holes with mincemeat, put a knob of butter on top and sprinkle with brown sugar.

5 Pour 3cm of water into the dish and bake in a preheated oven at 180°C, uncovered, for 40 minutes.

6 Serve hot with plenty of custard.

RICHARD'S WINES
TO SHARE AND PAIR
Birds in the Vines

Wild birds of prey soar over the vineyard: buzzards, kites, occasionally even a white-tailed eagle. They are a magnificent sight but also protectors of our crop from small mammals and starlings. Over the past decade we have made great strides with biodiversity at Nutbourne. Areas of wild flowers, cover crops down the vine-rows and undisturbed wetlands have steadily increased the insect population.

The insects attract more and more small birds including kingfishers, nightingales and woodpeckers. These in turn bring in the birds of prey: it really is the circle of life.

My brother works hard to reduce his farming impact on the land. His latest thing is to grow winter turnips in the vineyards for the sheep to feast on during the period when the vines are dormant. This keeps the animals in the vineyards longer, naturally fertilizing and regenerating the land.

The stand-out dish for me this month is the Fallow Deer Loin. I recommend a really special Tbilvino Mukuzani Special Reserve from Georgia, by the Black Sea. This wine is matured in French oak for 15 months to create a balanced and complex palate of tannins, dark fruit and vanilla. Georgia has a 6,000-year-old winemaking tradition, with vinification taking place in underground ceramic gourds.

POOR KNIGHTS OF WINDSOR WITH PORT CHANTILLY

SERVES 4

3 eggs

225g dark brown sugar

a pinch of ground cinnamon

a pinch of ground ginger

a pinch of salt

4 thick slices of stale bread, each cut into 3 pieces

50g butter

For the port chantilly

150ml double cream

50ml port

juice of ½ lemon

To serve

8 tsp Medlar Jelly

sugar, for dusting

coarse black pepper

There are a few long-forgotten puddings which are lovely to revisit – Poor Knights of Windsor is definitely one of them. The Poor Knights were around in the 14th century; they became impoverished by dedicating their lives to fighting for king and country. Those the king favoured were pensioned at Windsor Castle, where presumably a stale bread dessert was a favourite!

1 Whisk the eggs, sugar, cinnamon, ginger and salt together in a shallow dish. Place the bread pieces into the egg mixture and turn them over to soak up all the liquid.

2 Melt the butter in a heavy-based frying pan over a moderate heat. Fry a few of the bread pieces at a time for about 1 minute on each side, until golden, lift them out on to a baking tin ready to bake.

3 Whip the cream to a folding consistency, continue to whip while adding the port and lemon juice. Set aside until ready to serve.

4 Before serving, reheat the toasts for 5 minutes in an preheated oven at 180°C. Serve with the port chantilly and 2 tsp of Medlar Jelly (see page 178). Finish with a dusting of icing sugar and a couple of twists of freshly ground black pepper.

THE DINNER TABLE

This unusual painting depicts a dinner table from above before food is served. Bridget has used a mixture of collage and painting. The canvas provides a strong sense of dining ritual, shape and anticipation.

WINTER

The countryside is stark and beautiful, most of the trees and plants are dormant, biding their time, just surviving. Having dogs to walk ensures you get outdoors in all the weather: there are the dramatic days of driving rain, sleet or blizzards making you feel intrepid to be out at all; and there are days which lift our hearts – a bright hoar-frost or newly fallen virgin snow with brilliant blue sky above. Winter is a time for reflection, re-assessing, cosy evenings sitting by a log fire with an interesting book, plus there is plenty of time for good home-cooking, good wine and good company.

THE VINEYARD IS AT PEACE

The vines are resting. Perhaps there is a whisper from the breeze, the sound of sheep chomping beneath the trellis, or an occasional bird call, but little else to disturb. We have many solitary hours of pruning to focus on.

There are over 27,000 vines at Nutbourne, and each must be assessed and pruned individually. It requires concentration and a sympathetic eye. We are looking for strong new canes to be the base for next season's crop. We reject the spindly ones because they might fail and the fat ones are likely to devote their energy to maintaining their own bulk, so it is something specific we are searching for. Each vine is pruned down to the trunk and just one or two canes and a maximum of 16 buds; everything else is cut out.

The real joy of pruning is that there is no time to think about anything else: you are in the zone, working with the vines, and the hours just slip past.

The winter is also the time to tackle some of the other tasks on the land: new deer fencing, trellis repairs, the construction of new sheds and new planting. A vineyard yields best between year six and year 30. After this the vines grow a little tired and, although the depth of flavour can be fantastic from old vines, it is good commercial practice to grub up and replant. Nutbourne is an old vineyard by UK standards, with some of our treasured planting well over 40 years old. Gregory and I discuss which blocks need replacing and which varieties we should plant in their place. It takes five years for a new vine to achieve proper production, so these are challenging decisions. How will wine-drinking trends change? What are competitors growing? Will there be over-supply of certain varieties? In the end you make your choices and live by them.

IN THE WINERY

The tanks and barrels are monitored daily as the wine inside slowly matures and develops. An oak barrel allows some gentle oxidization, to enhance the wine and also give it character from both the wood and the 'toasting' that a cooper has applied to the inside. We spend time as a family tasting, debating, then eventually blending individual batches to make something with greater balance and complexity. I always compare winemaking to cooking: there is no right or wrong answer – it is personal taste, experience and a bit of luck to make something truly outstanding.

The winter months are a time when trade customers come to visit, taste and negotiate new buying deals. We sometimes have to turn down new enquiries: the limitation of our single estate production means we cannot supply multiples or supermarkets. We did have an entertaining and slightly comical day tasting our wines with a delegation of wine importers from Japan. Language was a barrier, but the enjoyment and camaraderie of drinking wine together was not. We all hit it off. I am pleased to say that Nutbourne wines are now sold in certain restaurants and wine merchants across Japan.

WINTER CELEBRATIONS

The famous quote from Madame Bollinger is: 'I drink it when I'm happy and when I am sad. Sometimes I drink it when I am alone. When I have company, I consider it obligatory. I trifle with it if I'm not hungry and drink it when I am. Otherwise I never touch it – unless I'm thirsty.'

I think the same principle applies to gathering, eating together and enjoying a glass of English wine in the winter: basically, any excuse will do.

Christmas is, of course, the biggest annual celebration in the western world, and let's not pretend it is just Christmas Day. The festivities seem to kick off in late November and go right through until after Hogmanay. Our restaurants in London do more business than at any other time of year. (They need to before the abstemious months of the early new year.) It is also a fabulous time for family entertaining. Every family has its own traditions, but we hope some of our menu ideas for yuletide will help you develop new ones.

For the Gladwins, there are plenty of reasons to celebrate in January and February as well: birthdays, reunions and Burns Night. Even Shrove Tuesday gives us an opportunity for a pancake party. We love to try out different foods and unusual wines from all round the globe. And naturally, we don't give up on our fixation with cooking and eating out of doors whenever it proves possible.

WINTER COOKING

This divides into the festive season and the rest. We all want to serve food that is celebratory and a little bit indulgent at Christmas time. The champion ingredients such as cranberries, clementines and even Brussels sprouts must be included. We particularly recommend the Potted Goose, or an amazing vegan pan-roasted cauliflower dish, or the Fir Cone Chocolate Ganache. For a culinary challenge (and applause at the end of the day), we have given step-by-step instructions for a magnificent Venison Wellington. Or if you want a traditional alternative to plum pudding, try the Yuletide Strudel.

Wines too... feel free to totally ignore our suggestions but we have enjoyed making recommendations for some good Christmas drinking.

Into January we should not ignore the specialities of the season and ingredients growing in the wild. Forage for winter cress, wood sorrel or chickweed. Experiment with recipes such as Bridget's Raw Marmalade, Jerusalem Artichoke Shells or nettle white butter sauce. The long dark evenings mean there is time to challenge yourself with recipes that are a little more complicated: let me tempt you to try the Spiced Hogget or a classic Steak & Oyster Pie. Desserts are also an excellent pick-me-up in what are considered to be the most depressing months of the year: cheer up with a Trinity Burnt Cream in January or a Toffee Ginger Pudding in February.

COMPLEXITY IN WINE, SIMPLICITY IN ART

Bridget is again using collage for this striking new body of work: birds, trees, patterns and landscapes cut or torn, then overlapped into intricate, random designs. The image above will appear on Nutbourne's Nutty Blanc de Blancs 2018 Sparkling Wine to be released in the summer of 2024.

December

A spectrum of scents, flavours and traditions encapsulating the festive season – clementine, horseradish, pine needles, cranberries, smoked fish and slow-cooked goose.

THIS MONTH'S FOOD CHAMPIONS	SOURCE	CHARACTER & COMMENT	RECIPES
Brussels sprouts and winter greens	all greengrocers, or grow your own	textured, fresh, minty	December Salad, Mackerel Croquettes
cranberries	all greengrocers – now synonymous with Christmas	tangy, fruity, distinctive	Fir Cone Chocolate, Potted Goose, Cauliflower Steak
smoked mackerel	all fishmongers	oily, rich, smoky	Mackerel Croquettes
lovage	farmers' markets, or grow your own	celery, spicy, herbaceous	Cauliflower Steak
goose	good butchers	fatty, dark, wholesome	Potted Goose
horseradish	farmers' markets, specialist greengrocers or grow your own	fiery, strong, spicy	Mackerel Croquettes, Venison Wellington
walnuts	all good stores	a part of Christmas: slightly bitter, nutty, wholesome	December Salad, Cauliflower Steak, Yuletide Strudel
Douglas fir	forage	lemony, fruity, Christmassy	Fir Cone Chocolate
clementines	all good greengrocers	another taste of Christmas: tangy, sweet, citrussy	Christmas Gammon, Fir Cone Chocolate
apple brandy	specialist stores – choose English	woody, abundant apples, fierce	Potted Goose, Fir Cone Chocolate & a shot for the chef

POTTED GOOSE WITH ORANGE, CRANBERRY & CHESTNUTS

Goose is fantastic meat to eat, especially if the birds have been grass-grazed outdoors throughout the summer and autumn. Geese prepare themselves for winter scarcities by holding a large quantity of high-quality fat that can be cooked at a high temperature, hence the trend for goose fat roast potatoes. These days it seems to be quite rare to have roast goose on Christmas Day, but it is a shame to miss out on this glorious meat altogether, so we are proposing potted goose as a festive starter. Potted means cooked and preserved in fat. The meat is served with a tangy orange, cranberry and chestnut relish. It really does taste of Christmas. A starter like this suits a lighter style red wine. Try a Gamay or a Grenache or even our very own Pinot Noir.

1 Begin by making a dry marinade. Mix the sugar, salt, orange zest and coriander seeds together in a bowl. Rub this on to the goose leg and leave to marinate in the fridge overnight.

2 The next day, preheat the oven to 130°C. Clean off the marinade, put the goose into a roasting tin with the butter, cover with foil and cook in the oven for 4 hours. The flesh will become very tender, falling off the bone.

3 Retain the cooking fat for the 'potting'. As soon as the goose is cool enough to handle, pick the meat off the bone into a bowl. Discard the skin, sinews and bones.

4 Transfer the cooking fat to a small pan over a gentle heat, cook the garlic for a couple of minutes and season with salt and pepper.

5 Add the mixed spice and apple brandy to the goose meat, then stir in 3 tbsp of the hot goose fat. Taste for both richness and seasoning and add more fat, salt or pepper, if necessary.

6 Pack the mixture into individual ramekin dishes, pour a little extra fat on the top, then place the ramekins in the fridge to set. (Be sure to save the remaining goose fat as it is great for those famous roast potatoes.)

7 Prepare the relish by mixing the oranges, cranberries, chestnuts and parsley together with vinegar and black pepper. Allow the mixture to infuse for an hour or so before serving.

8 When ready to serve, dip the ramekins into hot water, run a knife round the edge and turn out on to individual plates. Serve the relish alongside, finish with fresh herbs and accompany with plenty of warm sourdough toast.

SERVES 4–6 AS A STARTER

60g caster sugar

60g salt

zest of 2 oranges

2 tsp coriander seeds

1 goose leg

80g unsalted butter

1 garlic clove, crushed

salt and freshly ground black pepper

1 tsp ground mixed spice

2 tbsp apple brandy

fresh herbs, to garnish

sourdough toast, to serve

For the relish

2 oranges, peeled and segmented

2 tbsp dried cranberries

2 tbsp cooked chestnuts, chopped

1 tbsp chopped parsley

1 tbsp sherry vinegar

DECEMBER SALAD: BRUSSELS SPROUTS, APPLE, MATURE CHEDDAR & CANDIED WALNUTS

SERVES 6

1 tbsp honey

50ml rapeseed oil

sea salt and freshly ground black pepper

150g walnuts

400g Brussels sprouts

2 Cox's apples

150g grated mature Cheddar cheese

juice of 2 lemons

This dish has been a favourite in the Gladwin Brothers' restaurants for many years. It is a delectable, simple marriage of wholesome winter ingredients; we are delighted to share the recipe again.

1 Preheat the oven to 160°C. Mix the honey with half the oil and plenty of seasoning; add the walnuts and toss until they are thoroughly coated in the mixture. Transfer them to an ovenproof dish, place in the oven and bake for 8 minutes (or use an air fryer).

2 Remove and discard the outer leaves from the sprouts; shred the sprouts. Core the apples and cut them into matchsticks.

3 Mix the sprouts, apples and cheese in a bowl, add the lemon juice and the remaining oil, then toss together.

4 Arrange the salad in a serving dish, with the walnuts and honey on top.

OLIVER'S TALES FROM A FORAGER'S DIARY
Never Eat the Red Berries

Throughout my life I have always loved exploring off the beaten track, through the undergrowth, down the course of a hidden stream or into dense woodland, to discover nature's untouched treasures. It's a thrill like nothing else and still gives me butterflies in my stomach.

Our ancestors were hunter-gatherers with great knowledge of what could or could not be used from the wild. This connection to nature is more than just a hobby: it's my passion. Often, I find ingredients you just can't buy to bring home to my kitchen.

One of my earliest childhood memories was climbing the big yew tree in our garden, hiding in the branches, observing nature

(and my brothers). I remember Mum saying, 'Never eat the red berries, they are deadly poisonous.' Yew berries look like pretty red sweeties to a child. I have since learned that the flesh of the yew fruit is edible and it is the seed that is poisonous – but I don't recommend you try it.

PAN-ROASTED CAULIFLOWER STEAK, CRANBERRY, WALNUT & LOVAGE SALSA

For me this is the ultimate vegan Christmas dinner. There is great contrast between the wholesome texture of the roasted cauliflower and the nutty, creamy purée. The salsa, with its sweet cranberries, crunchy walnuts, savoury lovage and a good kick of red chilli, is the perfect companion. A vegan dish can be popular with omnivores and herbivores alike: we can highly recommend this as something a little different for a seasonal dinner party. Alternatively, if you are wedded to serving your roast turkey, the pan-roasted cauliflower is a perfect dish to prepare in advance and then present to any vegan guests – they will be bowled over!

SERVES 3–4

1 medium cauliflower, outer leaves removed

75ml rapeseed oil

½ garlic clove

50ml almond milk

a pinch of ground nutmeg

salt and freshly ground black pepper

For the salsa

100g dried cranberries

75g shelled walnuts, broken

a small bunch of lovage, stems removed, chopped

1 red chilli, thinly sliced

juice of 1 lemon

marigold petals and lovage sprigs, to decorate

1 Place the cauliflower, stem down, on a chopping board and use a serrated knife to carefully cut three or four 2cm-thick steaks across the full profile. Take out the middle of the stems and discard these.

2 Cut the cauliflower offcuts into florets. Bring a pan of lightly-salted water to boil over a moderate heat and cook the florets (not the steaks) for 15 minutes, then drain through a colander.

3 While still hot, transfer the cooked cauliflower to a food processor, add 1 tbsp of the rapeseed oil, the garlic and the almond milk. Season with nutmeg, salt and pepper, then blitz to a smooth purée. Keep the purée warm or set aside to reheat later.

4 Prepare the salsa. Place the cranberries, walnuts, chopped lovage and chilli slices together in a small bowl, add the lemon juice and 2 tbsp of the oil and season well with salt. Leave at room temperature, to macerate and develop flavour.

5 Heat a heavy-based frying pan over a high heat and add a little of the remaining oil. When smoky hot, sear the cauliflower steaks for about 2 minutes on each side: you want some nicely singed colour. Do this for one or two steaks at a time, adding a little extra oil each time. Transfer the steaks to an ovenproof dish, ready to roast when required.

6 When you are ready to serve, preheat the oven to 170°C. Finish the cauliflower by cooking in the oven for 6–8 minutes. Reheat the purée in the oven at the same time, in an ovenproof dish covered with foil.

7 Use piping hot plates for serving. Place a cauliflower steak in the centre of each plate, spoon small mounds of cauliflower purée around, then drizzle the salsa over. Decorate with extra lovage and marigold petals if you still have some.

SMOKED MACKEREL CROQUETTES, PICKLED WINTER SALAD, HORSERADISH CREAM

SERVES 4

For the horseradish cream

2 tbsp grated horseradish

100ml crème fraiche

1 lemon, zest and juice

a small bunch of chives, chopped

salt and freshly ground black pepper

For the béchamel

20g butter

20g plain flour

100ml milk

1 heaped tbsp grated horseradish

a pinch of ground nutmeg

½ tsp English mustard

For the croquettes

100g cooked potato, mashed (and dry)

200g smoked mackerel fillet, skinned and flaked

2 tbsp flour

1 egg, beaten

50g panko breadcrumbs

500ml sunflower oil, for frying

For the salad

100g winter greens, shredded

1 daikon radish, spiralized into strips

1 head of radicchio, shredded

1 tbsp virgin rapeseed oil

1 tbsp red wine vinegar

1 tbsp brown sugar

Where we are in West Sussex there are actually very few genuinely good restaurants. You may think that I am just fussy, but my feeling is that, at today's prices, 'ok' is just not good enough; we might as well do it better and cheaper at home. A stark exception to this is a superb restaurant run by Lee and Liz Parsons. They take great pride in everything they do, Lee is an outstanding cook, and among his broad repertoire he often serves excellent croquettes: light, crisp, moist and flavoursome. This recipe is dedicated to The Parsons Table in Arundel – may it continue to flourish for many years.

1 Begin by making the horseradish cream. In a small bowl, combine the freshly grated horseradish with the crème fraiche, lemon juice and chives. Season well with salt and pepper.

2 Prepare the béchamel sauce. Heat the butter in a heavy-based pan over a moderate heat, stir in the flour, cook for one minute, stirring, until smooth. Blend in the milk and continue to cook until the mixture reaches boiling point. Remove the pan from the heat, stir in the horseradish, nutmeg and mustard, then season with salt and pepper.

3 While it is still warm, combine the béchamel with the mashed potato and the mackerel in a mixing bowl, then allow to cool completely.

4 Set the flour, egg and breadcrumbs out on three separate plates. Divide the fish mixture into 8 even amounts. Roll into rounds in the palms of your hands, then roll in the flour, followed by the egg and finally the breadcrumbs. Transfer the croquettes on to a tray and chill in the fridge until ready to cook.

5 Prepare the salad. Bring a pan of lightly-salted water up to the boil over a moderate to high heat. Add the greens, blanch for 3 minutes, then drain, refresh under the cold tap and drain again. Combine the greens with the raw daikon and radicchio, dress with oil, vinegar and sugar, season with salt and pepper.

6 When you are ready to serve, heat the cooking oil in a heavy-based pan over a moderate heat to a temperature of 180°C. Cook the croquettes for 5 minutes, turning them with a slotted metal spoon, until golden brown. Lift out on to kitchen paper to absorb any excess oil.

7 Serve the croquettes hot on a bed of pickled winter salad with a dollop of horseradish cream on top.

CHRISTMAS GAMMON WITH STEM GINGER, STAR ANISE & CHARGRILLED CLEMENTINE

Some years, Gregory rears a batch of heritage Saddleback pigs. They feast on acorns and hazelnuts in a natural free-range environment – there is nothing quite like it for succulent pork. In the late summer some were cured as gammon joints and sold at the vineyard Cellar Door. We produced both 'green' gammon and joints smoked over vine logs. Don't worry, this is not a hard sell: British gammon from any good butcher will work equally well in this spicy, festive recipe. Meat like this calls for big-bodied red wine – an Australian Shiraz, Cabernet Sauvignon from the US or an Italian Barolo.

SERVES 8–10

3kg boneless smoked gammon joint

2l ginger beer

1l clementine juice (or orange juice)

2 red onions, cut into quarters

20 cloves

2 cinnamon sticks

6 whole star anise

2 bay leaves

1 jar of stem ginger in syrup, the pieces cut into slivers

6 small clementines

2 tsp English mustard

juice of 1 or 2 lemons

freshly ground black pepper

flat-leaf parsley

1 Put the gammon joint into a large saucepan, pour over the ginger beer and clementine juice. Add the onions, 5 cloves, the cinnamon, star anise and bay leaves. If necessary, top up the pan with water to ensure that the meat is completely covered.

2 Place the pan on a moderate heat, bring to the boil, cover with a lid, then reduce the heat and simmer for 2 hours, topping up with water when necessary, to keep the joint covered in liquid.

3 Remove the gammon from the cooking liquor, allow to cool for a few minutes, then carefully cut off the skin, leaving just a thin layer of fat. Score the fat on the outside of the joint to create a diamond pattern. Stud this with the remaining cloves and push the ginger slivers into the scored cuts. Brush the whole joint with the stem ginger syrup.

4 Place the joint in a roasting tin with 500ml of the cooking liquor and bake in the oven for 20 minutes. After this time, reduce the oven temperature to 175°C, baste the joint and bake for a further hour. Cover the gammon with tin foil if it starts to singe.

5 Cut each of the clementines in half and place the halves, cut-side down, on a hot griddle for 2 minutes. Add these to the roasting tin for the last 10 minutes of cooking.

6 Remove the gammon and clementines from the tin, keep warm to rest before carving. Meanwhile, place the roasting tin directly on to a hot hob, add a little more of the cooking liquor and bring to a rapid boil to make the jus. Stir in the English mustard, lemon juice and black pepper, reduce the liquid, taste and season.

7 Carve the gammon into thin slices and serve the clementines on top. Spoon the jus over and finish with parsley. Joyeux Noël!

VENISON WELLINGTON, HORSERADISH EMULSION

SERVES 6–8 (WITH SECOND HELPINGS)

1.2kg venison fillet, trimmed

salt and freshly ground black pepper

a drizzle of rapeseed oil

For the onion compote

3 red onions, sliced

80g raisins

1 tsp ground mixed spice

80ml port

For the pancakes

50g plain flour

a pinch of salt

1 egg

2 tbsp chopped fresh herbs, such as parsley, chervil or basil

100ml milk

For the crust

400g ready-rolled puff pastry

flour, for dusting

1 egg, beaten

For the emulsion

40ml white wine vinegar

juice of 1 lemon

150g butter

4 egg yolks

1 tbsp Dijon mustard

2 tbsp horseradish relish

If you want to get away from turkey or goose for Christmas, there is no better celebratory dish than a Venison Wellington. And thank the Lord that supermarkets have not yet come up with a bland, mediocre, ready-to-bake version to spoil the efforts of hard-working chefs! This lovely recipe combines succulent tender venison fillet with a red onion compote, then a layer of green herb pancake in addition to the crispy pastry crust. The pancake is a bit of extra work but well worth making, as it protects the pastry from becoming soggy. Our sauce is a horseradish emulsion, similar to hollandaise but with a bit of bite.

1 Season the venison with salt and pepper, rub with a little oil. Heat a heavy-based dry pan over a high heat and sear the meat on all sides for 1–2 minutes. Remove from the pan and allow to cool.

2 Prepare the compote. Put the onion, raisins, spices and port into a small pan over a moderate heat, bring to the boil, reduce the heat, simmer until the wine has evaporated; allow to cool.

3 Make the pancakes. Whisk the flour, salt and egg together, add the milk and herbs, continue to whisk into a smooth batter.

4 Heat a non-stick pan over a moderate heat and rub with a little oil. Ladle in about a quarter of the pancake mix, cook one side, flip over and cook the other side. Transfer the pancake to a cooling rack, then repeat the process to make 3 more.

5 Flatten out the ready-rolled pastry on a floured work surface and trim to a rectangle measuring 30cm x 20cm.

6 Place the pancakes on the pastry to cover it completely, spoon the red onion mixture along the centre and place the venison on top.

7 Carefully wrap the pancake layer over the meat and tuck it in. Now wrap the pastry over to form a tight cylinder, seal the join with a dab of water, turn the parcel over, then tuck and seal the ends under.

8 Cut the pastry offcuts into 1cm-wide strips, brush them with water and lay them across the wellington in a lattice pattern. Glaze the pastry with beaten egg and transfer the wellington on to a baking tray lined with baking paper. Store in the fridge until ready for final cooking.

9 Prepare the emulsion. Put the vinegar and lemon juice into a small pan over a moderate heat, boil rapidly until reduced by half. Add the butter to the pan and stir until it has melted.

10 Put the egg yolks, mustard and horseradish relish into a bowl set over a pan of simmering hot water; season with salt and pepper. Beat the egg mixture with a hand whisk for one minute.

11 While still beating, slowly pour the hot butter mixture into the bowl a little at a time. Continue to beat until the sauce emulsifies and thickens, then taste and season again.

12 Remove the wellington from the fridge 30 minutes before cooking. Preheat the oven to 200°C. Roast the wellington in the oven for 20–25 minutes, until the pastry is golden brown.

13 Keep it warm, allowing it to rest for 20 minutes before carving and serving.

RICHARD'S WINES
TO SHARE AND PAIR
Big Bottles

They say that the best-sized bottle for traditional-method Champagne or sparkling wine is a magnum. This gives optimum space for the wine to mature during its secondary fermentation. There are much larger Champagne bottles available, but these are first made in magnums, then decanted at the finishing stage. Our family loves a big bottle; there is nothing better during the festive season. Sharing a jeroboam (four bottles) among a large group seems so much more celebratory than sharing the same volume of wine in single bottles. And somehow it tastes that much better too.

So my recommendations for Christmas drinking are big bottles of fizz to begin, tall magnums of Nutbourne's own Sussex Reserve with the December Salad or Potted Goose, then a jeroboam of Spanish Ribera del Duero, a Chianti Classico or Cru Bourgeois Bordeaux with the Venison Wellington. Last but not least, splash out on a half-bottle of exquisite Grand Cru Sauternes. Serve this in tiny, chilled glasses with the Yuletide Strudel – it will be just enough to go round and will taste like nectar itself on Christmas Day.

FIR CONE CHOCOLATE GANACHE, DOUGLAS FIR CREAM & CARAMELIZED CRANBERRIES

Emma made these fun fir cone-shaped chocolate mousses for our Christmas Pop-Up in the Barrel Room and I could not resist including them in this month's seasonal recipes. The pop-ups were held in a room full of oak barrels with vintage Chardonnay and Pinot Noir fermenting alongside the diners. If you listened hard you could hear a little tune of gently popping bubbles from the air valves at the top of each barrel – but the revellers were never that quiet! Douglas fir pine needles are a fashionable ingredient to use. Treat them in the same way as you would rosemary: allow the flavours to infuse, then sieve the actual needles out. To make this recipe you will need to invest in some plastic fir-cone moulds but they are not expensive and the result is a very stylish, in-vogue pudding. As for wine with this dessert, it must be English sparkling all the way – our own Nutty Vintage or the elegant Camel Valley Rosé from Cornwall.

SERVES 6

For the chocolate ganache

150ml milk

150ml double cream

40ml apple brandy

2 eggs

1 tbsp caster sugar

a pinch of sea salt

200g dark chocolate, grated or finely chopped

For the Douglas fir cream

1 tbsp fresh pine needles, stalks removed, plus some sprigs to decorate

2 tbsp muscovado sugar

200ml double cream

For the cranberries

100g fresh cranberries

3 tbsp caster sugar

2 clementines, peeled and segmented

1 Make the ganache. Put the milk, cream and brandy into a heavy-based saucepan over a gentle heat and bring to scalding point.

2 Put the eggs, sugar and salt together in a mixing bowl, beat for one minute, pour in the hot milk mixture, beat together then pour the mixture back into the saucepan. Place over a low heat and stir continuously until thickened.

3 Now add the grated chocolate to the bowl, pour the hot mixture over and stir until the chocolate is melted.

4 Place the fir-cone moulds on a flat baking sheet, pour the ganache evenly into each mould, place in the fridge and chill overnight.

5 Prepare the Douglas fir cream. Put the muscovado sugar and pine needles into a small pan over a gentle heat and allow the sugar to melt without stirring, set aside to infuse.

6 Whip the cream until it holds, pour the melted sugar through a sieve into the cream. Discard the pine needles. Stir the mixture and place in the fridge to chill until required.

7 Place the cranberries, sugar and clementine segments in a small saucepan over a low heat, bring to the boil, then reduce the heat and simmer for about 5 minutes, until the liquid has evaporated and the cranberries are soft and tender.

8 Un-mould the chocolate fir cones and arrange them on individual plates. Serve the cranberry compote and cream alongside and decorate with a sprig of Douglas fir.

YULETIDE STRUDEL: APPLE, MINCEMEAT, WALNUTS & CRANBERRIES

SERVES 6

For the fruit filling

3 Granny Smith apples, peeled, cored and cut into chunks

3 tbsp Grandmother's Mincemeat (see page 188)

1 lemon, zest and juice

100g chopped walnuts

200g dried cranberries

2 tsp ground cinnamon

a pinch of salt

For the pastry

320g ready-rolled puff pastry

1 egg

a splash of milk

a pinch of salt

demerara sugar, for sprinkling

To serve

icing sugar, for dusting

custard, whipped cream or ice cream

Salzburg, Austria is a haven of Christmas markets, and everyone appears to eat strudel at all times of the day. Each restaurant and café competes for the best. Having experienced a trip there, Bridget and I feel compelled to offer our own strudel recipe for Christmas.

1 Put the apple, mincemeat and lemon into a heavy-based saucepan over a gentle heat, cook slowly for 5 minutes, stirring occasionally. Stir in the walnuts, cranberries, cinnamon and salt, set the mixture aside to cool.

2 Lay out a rectangular sheet of puff pastry and pile the fruit mixture down the centre. Make parallel angled cuts on both exposed sides of the pastry. These need to run at opposite angles on each side of the fruit, like a chevron pattern.

3 Fold the pastry strips over the fruit mixture, one at a time, from alternative sides, to form a plait, sealing each strip with a dab of water.

4 Transfer the strudel to the prepared baking tin lined with baking paper. Mix the egg with a little salt and milk, brush this on to the strudel, then sprinkle the top with demerara sugar.

5 Bake in a preheated oven at 200°C for 35 minutes, until golden brown. Serve warm with whipped cream or custard.

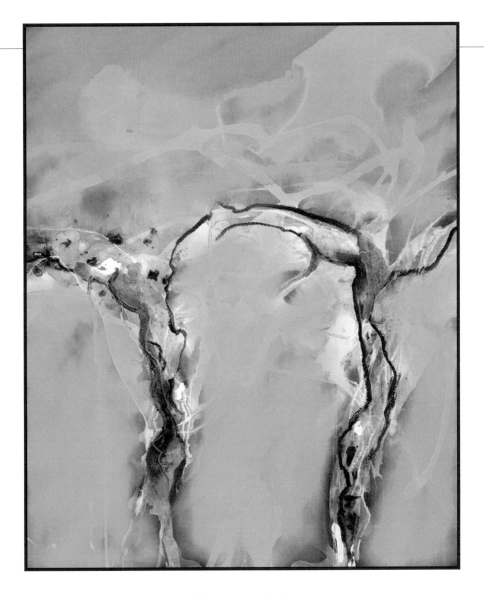

NUTTY VINTAGE BRUT

This painting is a partner to the Nutty Wild image on page 113, but with the glorious colouring of translucent deep-sea water. The vines appear to float in the background – free, ancient, structural and bold.

This image has become synonymous with our premium sparkling wine, classic-method Nutty Vintage Brut, where it is always featured on the label.

January

A time for the robust flavours of slow braised beef, spiced hogget, or pheasant with winter kale, cabbages and celeriac, as well as foraging in the woods for those edibles hidden in the depths.

THIS MONTH'S FOOD CHAMPIONS	SOURCE	CHARACTER & COMMENT	RECIPES
celeriac	all good greengrocers, or grow your own	earthy, nutty, celery	January Salad
kale and kalettes	farmers' markets, or grow your own	pleasant, sweet, textured	January Salad, River Trout
Seville oranges	imported in January only	very tart, great for cooking	Raw Marmalade
last of the game birds	shoots, game dealers, specialist butchers	flavoursome, getting tougher late in the season	Poacher's Soup
winter herbs and leaves	forage for winter cress, thyme, chickweed, wood sorrel, wild sage	wild, hardy, aromatic	Poacher's Soup, Tarte Tatin, Spiced Hogget
hogget	farm shops, specialist butchers	tender, smoky, rich	Spiced Hogget
river trout	good fishmongers or catch your own	light, flaky, sweet, rivery	River Trout
beetroot	farmers' markets, greengrocers	sweet, earthy, fulsome	Tarte Tatin
fennel tops	forage or grow your own	aniseed, herby, fresh	River Trout

JANUARY SALAD: CELERIAC, KALETTES, PINK GRAPEFRUIT & CAESAR DRESSING

Start the New Year with a special vegan salad. The raw celeriac must be thinly shaved to avoid it being too woody, and we recommend kalettes – a hybrid of kale and Brussels sprouts – to ensure the greens are tender. This recipe also uses ground cashew nuts in place of egg as the base for Caesar dressing – it can be used for lots of different vegan dishes. For 'dry January', we recommend a dry white wine: Pinot Grigio, Orvieto or Austrian Grüner Veltliner.

1 Begin by making the garlic croutons. Cut the sourdough into small chunks. Heat the oil in a medium-sized, heavy-based frying pan over a moderate heat, toss in the bread and garlic and fry for 2–3 minutes, until golden. Drain on kitchen paper.

2 Prepare the vegan Caesar dressing. Put the nuts, garlic, lemon juice, mustard and Parmesan into a food processor and blitz to a smooth paste. With the blade still running, pour in the oil, a little at a time. When it has all emulsified, taste, season with salt and cayenne pepper and taste again.

3 Shave the celeriac with a wide-mouthed peeler. Place the shavings in a bowl of lightly-salted cold water with the remains of the squeezed lemon until ready to use.

4 Drain the celeriac from the water, dab it dry on kitchen paper, then combine with the kalettes and spinach leaves in a serving dish. Scatter the grapefruit segments, capers and croutons on top and finish with the Caesar dressing.

SERVES 4–6

For the croutons
2 slices of sourdough bread
2 tbsp sunflower oil
1 garlic clove, crushed

For the Caesar dressing
50g raw cashew nuts
1 garlic clove, crushed
juice of 1 lemon
1 tbsp Dijon mustard
2 tbsp vegan Parmesan
100ml rapeseed oil
salt and cayenne pepper

For the salad
1 celeriac, peeled
150g kalettes
100g baby spinach
2 pink grapefruit, peeled and segmented
1 tbsp capers

OLIVER'S TALES FROM A FORAGER'S DIARY
January Pennywort

I have gathered pennywort in the wild all my chef years: it is a perennial edible plant that has no aroma but fleshy herbaceous leaves, tasting like a cross between cucumber, parsley and asparagus. The plant grows in damp, rocky lanes but also on some shady tree trunks. The more you pick from a patch, the more it spreads.

One day, I visited a patch along a quiet country lane. It is a place where I have been foraging for years. Suddenly a large hunting horse came galloping up to me with a fierce-looking lady in the saddle. She demanded to know what I was up to with her pennywort. I was impressed she knew what it was but the look on her face, mounted high above me, gave the clear impression that this was not the moment for a nice chat about wild herbs and foraging!

She firmly explained that she had brought this plant over from Jersey many years ago, it was growing on the boundary of her land and it was her crop. Then she trotted off.

I did manage to use these special leaves for a dish that day, so this can be a thank-you to the lady on the horse. It turns out, of course, that Mum and Dad know her and say she is very nice!

GAME POACHER'S SOUP WITH WILD HERB DUMPLINGS

SERVES 6

1 or 2 game birds: partridge, pheasant, woodcock or wild duck

1 onion, quartered

2 carrots, halved lengthways

a bunch of celery tops, cut into 10cm lengths

bay leaves, wild thyme and parsley

3 tbsp sherry vinegar

salt and freshly ground black pepper

200g Savoy cabbage, shredded

a good slug of Scotch whisky

For the dumplings

200g self-raising flour, plus extra for dusting

a pinch of salt

50g cold butter, grated

2 tbsp chopped wild sage, wood sorrel and winter cress

6 tbsp cold water

Poachers could not be fussy about the game they 'found' in the landowner's woodland. Sometimes it would be rabbits, hare or venison and, at other times, partridge, pheasant or other wild birds. This recipe is perfect for using any extra game birds 'happened upon in the country-side' or, more realistically, forgotten in your freezer. Also, in the last month of the shooting season, the birds are often a bit tougher, so slow boiling to make a delicious, meaty broth is the answer. The wild-herb dumplings are a lovely addition. If you look carefully on the woodland floor you should find wild sage, wood sorrel and winter cress but, if not, use any fresh herbs from the greengrocer.

1 Put the game birds into a large saucepan with the onion, carrot, celery tops, bay leaves, wild thyme and parsley. Fill the pan with cold water to cover, add the vinegar and season well with salt and pepper. Put a lid on the pan, place over a high heat and bring to the boil, then reduce the heat and simmer for 1 hour.

2 Meanwhile, prepare the dumplings. Rub the flour, salt and butter together in a mixing bowl until the mixture resembles breadcrumbs. Add the wild herbs and water, then bring the dough together with your fingertips. Do not overwork it. Flour your hands and roll the dough into even-sized balls in your palms. Set them aside, ready to cook.

3 Carefully lift the game birds out of the stock, allow them to cool enough to handle, then pull the flesh off the bones. Discard the skin and bones, then cut the meat into strips and set aside.

4 Sieve the vegetables and herbs out of the stock and discard them. Return the pan of stock to the stove over a moderate heat. As it comes up to the boil, drop in the dumplings and cook them for 10 minutes. Stir in the shredded cabbage and continue to cook for another 3–4 minutes.

5 Finally, add the game meat to the pan, simmer for a couple of minutes, add a slug of whisky and serve.

BRIDGET'S RAW CITRUS MARMALADE

Seville oranges are only in the markets during January – so don't miss the opportunity to use them. This simple uncooked marmalade recipe makes a lovely, fresh citrus conserve with a wide variety of uses. Serve it on toast, with yoghurt, as a topping for cakes, to sharpen up a savoury dish, or take a jar to friends as an unexpected winter gift.

**MAKES APPROXIMATELY
6 X 350 ML JARS**

4 Seville oranges

4 clementines

2 large oranges

2 lemons

1 pink grapefruit

1.5kg caster sugar
(approximate weight)

1 Wash and dry the whole fruits. Cut each one into large pieces and remove all the pips. In batches, put the fruit into a food processor and blitz to a chunky pulp (not a liquid), then transfer it to a large mixing bowl.

2 Weigh the fruit. The amount of sugar needs to be ¾ of the weight of the fruit. Stir the correct amount of sugar into the pulped fruit.

3 Spoon the mixture into sterilized jars and seal the lids. Store in the fridge.

TIP Sterilizing the jars before use is essential for all jams, preserves, pickles or conserves. To do this, preheat the oven to 180°C. Place the clean, dry jars and lids upside-down on a baking tray and place in the oven for 20 minutes. Remove them and allow to cool before use.

BEETROOT & GOAT'S CHEESE TARTE TATIN

SERVES 6–8

For the filling

100g caster sugar

1 tsp red wine vinegar

salt and pepper

mixed spice

For the tart

500g cooked beetroot, sliced into discs

1 tsp chopped thyme

500g ready-made puff pastry

a little flour, for dusting

To finish

pennywort

beetroot leaves

wild herbs

2 tbsp rapeseed oil

100g goat's cheese, crumbled

This fabulous savoury winter version of the classic caramelized tart is made with beetroot and goat's cheese, then dressed with foraged leaves and herbs. A tarte tatin is cooked upside down in caramel to maximize the succulent flavour of its filling. The dish works equally well for a casual lunch or a grand dinner party starter.

1 Preheat the oven to 180°C. Heat the sugar in a small saucepan over a low heat: allow it to melt and then to caramelize to a deep golden colour.

2 Take the pan off the heat and add the vinegar, standing well back, as it will splutter. Season the caramel with salt, pepper and some mixed spice.

3 Pour the mixture into the bottom of a 20cm non-stick cake tin. Immediately place a neat layer of sliced beetroot on to the caramel, sprinkle with a layer of thyme, add the remaining beetroot slices and press down into the tin.

4 Roll out the pastry on a floured surface to form a 25cm circle. Place the pastry over the beetroot and tuck the sides down all round the edges.

5 Bake in the oven for 30 minutes, until golden brown.

6 Remove the tart from the oven and allow it to cool for 5 minutes, then run a round-ended knife around the edge to loosen it from the tin. Place a plate on top, turn the whole thing over as one, then lift off the tin.

7 Make a quick wild herb pesto in a food processor by blitzing together some of the foraged leaves and herbs, retaining some to decorate the finished tart. Season well, then drizzle in the oil while the blades are still running.

8 Reheat the tart before serving, then sprinkle with crumbled goat's cheese, dot with herb pesto and decorate with leaves and herbs.

RIVER TROUT, CAPERS, FENNEL TOPS & CAVIAR

It's a chilled but fair day in mid-January and the brothers and I have been clearing trees that have started to overshadow the vineyard. It is time for a lunch break! There is no reason why cooking on an open fire and outdoor eating has to be restricted to the summer months. The ever-inspired Oliver has the vision for trout cooked at the water's edge and Richard has brought down a bottle of our own Bacchus. The butter-fried smoky fish just melts in our mouths, with a burst of flavour from the capers and caviar. The Bacchus is crisp, aromatic and refreshing. Not a bad way to spend a weekday in January. We have adapted this recipe a little for home cooking. The caviar is an optional luxury, as is the Bacchus wine, but both are highly recommended.

SERVES 4

150g butter

4 whole rainbow trout, gutted, heads removed

100g kalettes, blanched for a few moments in boiling water

2 tbsp capers

salt and freshly ground black pepper

a splash of dry white wine

40g caviar

a bunch of fennel fronds

1 Melt half the butter in a large pan over a moderate heat. Add the trout to the pan and cook them with the skin on for about 5 minutes on each side.

2 When the fish are cooked, remove the skin. To do this, lift the skin at the head end and peel it off in one piece, then flip the fish over and skin the other side.

3 Keep the fish in the hot pan over the heat. Add the rest of the butter, the white wine, kalettes and capers, then season with salt and pepper.

4 Top the fish with black caviar and fennel fronds and serve right away. Some wood-fire-roasted jacket potatoes and a glass of wine are all you could wish for to go with it.

RICHARD'S WINES TO SHARE AND PAIR
The Rolling Stones of the Rhône Valley

We learn from other wine regions all the time: what creates their unique style and how things have developed over the centuries. The Gladwin restaurants have a special relationship with the Perrin family in southern Rhône. Our Sussex restaurant in Soho is twinned with their L'Oustalet restaurant in the village of Gigondas. I have therefore had several opportunities to explore this wonderful vine-growing region. The floor of the southern Rhône valley is clay with massive round stones that originally rolled down from the Alps.

Within the vineyards the stones bake in the hot sun by day then retain their heat to keep the soil warm at night, creating a superb environment for developing grapes for fabulous red wines.

So, let's try some fantastic Perrin wines to accompany the Spiced Hogget or wholesome Slow-cooked Beef. Choose from the Famille Perrin basic Côtes du Rhône, their smaller appellations of Vacqueyras and Gigondas, or the mighty Château de Beaucastel – considered to be one of the finest red wines in the world.

SPICED HOGGET, GOLDEN RAISINS, PISTACHIO AND POMEGRANATE

SERVES 4

1.2kg lamb shoulder, on the bone

40g sea salt

1 brown onion, cut in half

4 garlic cloves, cut in half

3 rosemary sprigs

4 whole star anise

1 cinnamon stick

2 tsp sumac

1 tbsp tomato purée

200ml red wine

200ml water

80g golden raisins

To garnish

50g shelled pistachios, chopped

seeds of 1 pomegranate

wild sage

January can be a depressingly long, dull month. As you can imagine, I am not a great believer in 'dry January' or, for that matter, any other campaigns to stop drinking wine, eating nice things and get depressed. What we need in January is some delicious, robust, wholesome cooking and an excuse to drink some well-aged fine Bordeaux wines. This slow-cooked one-to-two-year-old sheep is just the ticket. There is nothing politically incorrect about me!

1 Rub the lamb shoulder with the salt and refrigerate overnight.

2 The following day, heat the oven to 140°C. Brush off any excess salt from the lamb and put the joint in a deep roasting tin together with the onion, garlic, rosemary, spices, tomato purée, red wine and water.

3 Cover the tin with a layer of greaseproof paper and then with aluminium foil and place it in the oven. Cook for 4 hours.

4 Remove the roasting tin from the oven and, as soon as the lamb is cool enough to handle, strip the meat off the bone into strands, discarding any pieces of tough sinew.

5 Divide the cooked hogget meat into 4 equal amounts. Place four 8cm cooking rings on an oiled baking tray, place a portion of meat into each one and press down. Chill them in the fridge until ready to serve.

6 Place the tin of cooking juices on the hob over a high heat. Bring to a rapid boil and reduce by roughly half. Transfer all the juices into a small saucepan, discarding the onion and rosemary, but scrape out all the spice, garlic and goodness from the tin. Add the raisins to the pan, then set aside, ready to reheat and serve.

7 To serve, preheat the oven to 200°C. Bake the hogget for 12 minutes and reheat the sauce on the hob. Serve the meat on individual plates with the sauce spooned over. Scatter with pistachios, pomegranate seeds and wild sage.

SLOW-COOKED BEEF WITH MUSTARD CROUTES

SERVES 4–6

For the beef casserole

40g butter

200g small onions, blanched and peeled

200g button mushrooms

600g silverside of beef, trimmed and diced

40g plain flour

salt and freshly ground black pepper

500ml red wine

300ml water

2 tbsp dark brown sugar

2 tbsp red wine vinegar

1 tbsp Dijon mustard

For the mustard croutes

1 French stick

2 tbsp wholegrain mustard

To serve

parsley leaves

We understand the difference between fine wine and plonk, so why is there so little appreciation of the difference between hand-reared, grass-fed beef and the supermarket stuff? Gregory knows his cows by name, personally sees each calf into the world and feeds them on the best the land has to offer. The result is that the beef really tastes of something. This recipe for a braised beef topped with crunchy mustard seed croutes is a winter classic.

1 Melt the butter in a large cast-iron casserole dish over a moderate heat. Add the onions, cook until they are lightly browned all over. Add the mushrooms, cook for a further 2 minutes, lift out of the pan and reserve.

2 Roll the diced beef in seasoned flour. Add the meat to the hot casserole dish, brown on all sides for 2–3 minutes.

3 Add the red wine, water, sugar, mustard and vinegar to the casserole, stir in the onions and mushrooms, season again. Bring the mixture to the boil, put a lid on the dish, transfer to a preheated oven at 160°C. Cook for 2 hours.

4 Prepare the croutes. Cut the bread into 1.5cm-thick slices and spread each slice generously with wholegrain mustard.

5 After 2 hours, take the casserole out of the oven, remove the lid and arrange the croutes on top, making sure they are embedded in the liquid. Return the casserole to the oven and bake, uncovered, for a further 20 minutes. Sprinkle with parsley and serve.

FRUIT & NUT LOAF WITH MATURE CHEDDAR

This is something like Welsh bara brith – a moist, wholesome dairy-free loaf, providing nourishment and encouragement for a cold winter's day working among the vines.

1 Preheat the oven to 150°C. Oil a 500g loaf tin and line it with baking parchment.

2 Measure all the remaining ingredients, except the eggs and salt, into a large bowl and thoroughly mix together with a wooden spoon.

3 Lightly beat the eggs with a pinch of salt, then stir these into the mixture until well incorporated.

4 Spoon the cake mix into the prepared loaf tin, spread it evenly to the sides, then bake in the oven for 1 hour.

5 The cake will not rise – but you can check if it is cooked through by spiking it with a skewer; the skewer should come out clean. Turn the cake out on to a wire rack and allow to cool before serving.

6 Slice the cake and serve with cheese or butter. The cake will last for a good two weeks, stored in an airtight container.

MAKES 10–16 SLICES

oil, for greasing

40g plain flour

40g wholemeal flour

30g ground almonds

100g golden raisins

100g dried dates, stoned and chopped

100g dried apricots, chopped

80g walnuts, chopped

140g dark brown sugar

2 eggs

a pinch of salt

To serve

200g Cheddar cheese, or butter

TRINITY BURNT CREAM

SERVES 6

500ml double cream

1 vanilla pod, split, seeds scraped out

6 egg yolks

100g caster sugar

TIP The perfect Trinity Cream should be served warm on top from the grilling and with the custard beneath still chilled.

Every cookbook needs a crème brûlée recipe. The original comes from a crema catalana, which then evolved into the French classic. This was subsequently claimed by Trinity College Cambridge in the late 19th century as its signature dessert.

1 Put the cream and vanilla pod into a small heavy-based pan over a moderate heat. Bring up to scalding point, remove the pan from the heat. Allow the cream to infuse with the vanilla for 1 hour.

2 Whisk the egg yolks and 60g of caster sugar together in a large mixing bowl, set the bowl over a pan of simmering hot water to form a bain-marie. Pick out the vanilla pod from the cream, stir the cream into the egg mix, allowing the mixture to slowly cook and thicken, stirring occasionally. It will take about 20 minutes and will be ready when it can coat a wooden spoon.

3 Pour the mixture into six individual heatproof serving dishes, and place these in the fridge to chill.

4 When ready to serve, cover the tops of the Trinity Creams with a thin, even layer of sugar. Place them under a hot grill until the sugar melts, bubbles and turns a golden brown.

STILL LIFE & PINOT NOIR

Bridget has moved into a series of still-life canvasses, capturing a mix of obscure and everyday objects. We have used one of her still-life paintings to represent our Pinot Noir red wine. Like the painting, this is an unusual multi-faceted wine with dark stone fruit, autumnal character, warm spice and pleasing gentle tannins.

February

Cold grey days, pruning in the vines. The reward of hidden treasure dug from the veg patch –
Jerusalem artichokes, winter beetroots and heritage carrots.

THIS MONTH'S FOOD CHAMPIONS	SOURCE	CHARACTER & COMMENT	RECIPES
winter cress	forage along banks of streams	peppery, fresh, like watercress	February Salad
dulse seaweed	on the seashore, or dried in health stores	nutritious, deep-sea umami	Baked Cod
young nettles	foraging almost anywhere	tangy, fresh, herby – be careful how you handle them	Baked Cod
Jerusalem artichokes	good greengrocers or grow your own	earthy, nutty and sweet	Jerusalem Artichoke Shells
celeriac	specialist game dealers in season	dark, full-flavoured, lean and gamey	Hare Bonbons
hare	farm shops, specialist butchers	tender, smoky, rich	Hare Bonbons
forced rhubarb	farm shops, markets or your veg garden	sour, tangy, ample berry-style flavour	Toffee Pudding
oysters	good fishmongers	the taste of the sea: succulent, moreish	Steak & Oyster Pie
winter beetroots and carrots	good greengrocers or grow your own	sweet, earthy, nourishing	February Salad

PANCAKES GALORE

MAKES 10

For the batter

100g plain flour

salt

2 eggs

1 tbsp sunflower oil, plus extra for cooking

250ml milk

PANCAKE FILLING IDEAS

smoked salmon, shaved fennel & crème fraiche

roasted butternut, aubergine & hazelnut

fresh tomato, avocado & feta bound with pesto

grated apple, sultanas & cinnamon

blueberry, honey & praline with Greek-style yoghurt

It's that time of year again: Shrove Tuesday – a perfect excuse to demonstrate your tossing skills and serve crêpe-style pancakes with some delicious fillings.

1 Sieve the flour with a good pinch of salt into a mixing bowl. Make a well in the middle, pour in the eggs, oil and 100ml of the milk.

2 Use a wooden spoon to blend the liquid into the flour to form a smooth paste. Leave the mixture for 30 minutes to allow the flour to swell.

3 Add the remainder of the milk into the flour paste, whisk into a smooth batter.

4 Place a non-stick frying pan over a medium to high heat, grease it with a wad of kitchen paper soaked in oil. (This can be used again and again, and it avoids having excess oil in the pan.) When the pan is piping hot, ladle in a small quantity of the batter and tilt the pan round to get an even spread.

5 Cook the pancake for about 60 seconds until it begins to brown at the edges, shake the pan to loosen, then toss with a single vertical, circular flip.

6 Allow the pancake to cook for a further 30 seconds, then turn out on to a plate ready to fill.

JERUSALEM ARTICHOKE SHELLS

These little delicacies are an unusual winter treat. Presented in crispy shells made from the artichokes' own skins, this is a great way to enjoy the unadulterated, nutty, earthy flavour of this extraordinary root vegetable. For something completely different, serve the artichoke shells with a dry manzanilla sherry or our very own Nutbourne Barrel Reserve.

MAKES 8

4 Jerusalem artichoke tubers

1 tbsp crème fraiche

salt and freshly ground black pepper

40g hard English cheese, finely grated

1 Preheat the oven to 160°C. Scrub the artichokes in cold water to remove any grit from the skins.

2 Place a pan of lightly-salted water over a moderate heat, bring to the boil and cook the artichokes for 15 minutes, either in the water or in a steamer above.

3 Drain and leave until cool enough to handle. Cut the tubers lengthways and carefully scoop out the flesh from the skins into a small bowl.

4 Place the artichoke skins, cut side up, in an ovenproof dish and bake in the oven for 10 minutes (or use an air fryer), until they have dried out.

5 Mix the artichoke flesh with the crème fraiche and season well with salt and pepper. Fill the shells with the mixture, gently reheat, then sprinkle them with cheese and decorate with edible petals. Serve warm.

BAKED COD, DULSE SEAWEED TAPENADE, PARSNIP PURÉE

Seaweed and olives make a lovely combination in a tapenade. Okay, a black olive is not very 'local and wild' to Sussex, but for every rule there must be exceptions. This is a stunning dish, both visually and in terms of flavour – the strong umami flavour of the tapenade on succulent cod fillets works really well with the sweet parsnip purée and rich nettle tang of the white butter sauce. Treat yourself to a good Pouilly-Fumé from the Loire valley or a fresh coastal Chilean Chardonnay to go with it.

1 First, make the tapenade. Put all the ingredients into a food processor and pulse briefly to chop – but don't blend to a purée. Set aside for the crust.

2 Prepare the parsnip purée. Cook the parsnips in a pan of lightly-salted boiling water for 10 minutes, drain through a colander and allow to dry.

3 Transfer the parsnips to a food processor, add the crème fraiche, season with salt and pepper, and blitz. Keep warm or cool, ready to reheat in the oven when you cook the fish.

4 Prepare the butter sauce. Put the crème fraiche, vinegar, lemon juice and sugar in a small pan over a gentle heat, and heat gently until melted – but do not boil.

5 Put the butter in a mixing bowl, then pour the hot cream mixture over and stir until the butter has melted. Add the nettles, season with salt and pepper and keep warm or reheat over a bain-marie when needed.

6 When ready to serve, preheat the oven to 180°C. Place the cod pieces on an oiled ovenproof dish. Spread the tapenade across the top of each piece of fish, place the dish in the oven and bake for 8 minutes.

7 Place a swirl of parsnip purée on individual plates, place a piece of the cod on top, spoon the nettle butter around and garnish with some extra seaweed.

SERVES 4

For the fish

500g cod fillet, cut into 4 pieces

oil, for greasing

For the tapenade

50g dulse seaweed, chopped, plus extra for garnish

50g pitted black olives

20g capers

a small slice of sourdough bread, stale if possible

1 garlic clove, roughly chopped

1 lemon, zest and juice

freshly ground black pepper

20ml virgin rapeseed oil

For the parsnip purée

2 parsnips, peeled and cut into chunks

2 tablespoons crème fraiche

salt and pepper

For the nettle white butter

150ml crème fraiche

1 tbsp tarragon vinegar

1 tbsp lemon juice

½ tsp caster sugar

40g butter, at room temperature, cut into cubes

young nettle leaves, finely chopped

FEBRUARY SALAD: RED RICE, CARROT, BEETROOT & WILD LEAVES, TAHINI EMULSION

SERVES 4–6

500g red rice

salt

2 tbsp rapeseed oil

2 tsp sumac

300g heritage carrots, diced

300g heritage beetroots, diced

For the tahini emulsion

1 garlic clove

150ml rapeseed oil

1 tbsp golden syrup

75g tahini paste

2 tsp chopped thyme

juice of 1 lemon

50ml white wine

salt and freshly ground black pepper

To finish

beetroot leaves, winter cress and green herbs

Wow! What a colourful visual statement on a plate for healthy February eating – and it's vegan too. Red rice is referred to as yet another superfood, but to me that is just a marketing ploy. Most natural ingredients are 'super' in their own way: we just need a broad, balanced diet to make sure we get a wide variety of nutrients.

1 Place the rice in a colander and rinse under cold running water. Bring a large pan of lightly-salted water to the boil, add the rice and cook for 30 minutes. Drain through a sieve, rinse and drain again.

2 Place the rice in a bowl, add the sumac, then dress with 2 tbsp rapeseed oil. Leave to cool.

3 Dice then cook the carrots and beetroot for 6 minutes in another pan of lightly-salted boiling water, drain, refresh, allow to cool.

4 Prepare the tahini emulsion. Put the garlic in a small pan over a gentle heat with a dribble of the oil and cook for 2 minutes. Transfer to a food processor, add the golden syrup, tahini, thyme, lemon juice and white wine, then blitz together. Continue to run the blade while slowly adding all the remaining oil: the mixture will emulsify to a thick, yoghurt-like consistency. Season with salt and pepper, taste, then season again.

5 Make a bed of the sumac red rice on a serving dish, scatter the carrots and beetroot on top, spoon on dollops of the tahini emulsion, then finish with beetroot leaves, winter cress and green herbs.

OLIVER'S TALES FROM A FORAGER'S DIARY
First Rose of the Year

The primrose takes its name from the Latin, *prima rosa*; it is celebrated as the first flower of the new season, bringing the message that winter will at last come to an end and spring is just around the corner. These lovely, gently scented, pale yellow flowers grow in clusters along grassy banks and are perfect for delicate garnishes or even sprinkled loosely through a salad.

Appreciation of the outdoors and all that nature has to offer is such a wonderful thing. I take my young sons out exploring in all weathers. They are thrilled by the 'to-wit, to-whoo' of an owl in the woods and my answering shrill whistle, using a long blade of grass; or the damp aroma after February rain; or spotting a worm slithering its way across the path near a mossy hole where the badger lives.

It's all a very long way from busy hot kitchens and it's not just about gathering things to eat. The sounds, smells, atmosphere and glorious visual treats of the natural environment are the most valuable things we have in this world. There is nowhere I feel more at peace.

CELERIAC, WILD MUSHROOM & LENTIL 'LASAGNE'

Oliver has created this delicious vegan and gluten-free recipe as a celebration of celeriac – an amazing winter root vegetable full of fibre and nourishment. Thin slices of celeriac are used in place of the pasta sheets you normally expect in a lasagne. Then, a purée of the same vegetable creates a béchamel without any dairy or flour. The dish is layered with a tasty mushroom, spinach and lentil ragù. The lasagne can be prepared in advance or even frozen, uncooked.

1 For the wild mushroom ragù, put the oil in a heavy-based pan over a moderate heat. Cook the onion, garlic and thyme until soft. Add the fresh mushrooms, cook for a further 5 minutes.

2 Stir in the lentils, chopped tomato and dried mushrooms together with the water they have been soaked in. Season to taste, reduce the heat, simmer for 40 minutes, until the lentils are cooked and the mixture has reduced and thickened.

3 Take the pan off the heat, stir in the spinach, and allow to cool.

4 Make a vegetable stock. Sweat the celeriac trimmings, onion, garlic, bay, peppercorns and nutmeg in a little rapeseed oil. Add 500ml of water, season with salt and onion powder. Simmer over a gentle heat for 30 minutes, until the volume is reduced by half. Skim off any impurities from the top, sieve out the solids, and set the stock aside for making the béchamel.

5 Cut wide ribbons from one of the peeled celeriac, using a wide-mouthed peeler. Blanch the ribbons in salted boiling water for 3 minutes, refresh under cold running water, set aside.

6 Dice the second celeriac into 2cm cubes. Heat a little more oil in a pan over a moderate heat and fry the celeriac cubes until lightly golden and tender. Transfer into a food processor, blitz while slowly adding the stock and the vegan parmesan. It will become a smooth, creamy béchamel.

7 Spoon a layer of the ragù into a casserole dish. Layer celeriac ribbons on top, and add another layer of each. Spoon the béchamel over, then lay pieces of celeriac and sweet potato in a scalloped layer on top.

8 Bake in a preheated oven at 180°C for 30 minutes, garnished with chopped parsley.

SERVES 4–6

2 celeriac, scrubbed and peeled, the trimmings reserved for stock

rapeseed oil

1 onion, chopped

1 garlic clove

bay leaves, peppercorns and nutmeg

1 tsp onion powder

60g vegan parmesan

1 sweet potato, peeled and sliced

parsley, to garnish

For the wild mushroom and lentil ragù

2 tbsp rapeseed oil

1 onion, diced

1 garlic clove, crushed

1 tbsp chopped thyme

150g fresh mushrooms, diced

100g puy lentils

40g dried wild mushrooms, soaked in 200ml warm water

400g canned chopped tomatoes

salt and pepper

150g spinach

SUFFOLK HARE & ALE BONBONS

MAKES 20

1kg hare, jointed but on the bone

1 red onion, finely diced

a few sprigs of thyme, sage and parsley

150ml dark beer

salt and freshly ground black pepper

200g minced pork

1 slice of dry brown bread

1 tsp ground mixed spice

3 tbsp plain flour

2 eggs, beaten

200g panko breadcrumbs

sunflower oil, for shallow frying

Cox's Apple & Rosehip Chutney, or similar, to serve (page 165)

Hare is not easy to get hold of, but there are specialist wild meat suppliers who sell it in the permitted season between August and February. We get ours from East Anglia. It is a rare treat and well worth serving – dark, rich, succulent meat with the distinct taste of the wild. In this recipe we braise the hare and then combine it with some pork (to increase the fat content) before rolling into small fried 'bonbons'. The delicacy is packed with flavour and perfect served as a canapé or 'amuse-bouche'. I like to complement the Bonbons with the sweetness of Cox's Apple & Rosehip Chutney (see page 165) – but any sharp, fruity jam or chutney will work well. As for wine pairing, I fancy some fine vintage English sparkling. We keep a stock of our older vintages in the cellar: after about eight years, the fizz becomes softer and the acidity lessens but the wine becomes more sophisticated, with pronounced buttery and spice flavours, in the same way as vintage Champagne.

---

1 Preheat the oven to 180°C. Put the hare, onion, herbs and beer together in an ovenproof dish, season with salt and pepper, cover with foil, and cook in the oven for 45 minutes.

2 Remove the dish from the oven and leave until the meat is cool enough to handle, then strip the flesh off the bone into small pieces.

3 Transfer the cooked onion, herbs and cooking juices to a food processor, add the pork, bread, spice and seasoning, then pulse the processor to blend the mixture.

4 Transfer the mixture to a bowl, mix in the hare, then chill in the fridge for half an hour.

5 Put the flour, egg and breadcrumbs on three separate plates. Roll the meat mixture into small, even-sized balls in the palms of your hands. Coat them first in the flour, then in the egg and finally in the breadcrumbs. Place them on a tray to chill in the fridge before frying.

6 When ready to serve, heat a heavy-based pan over a moderate heat with 5mm of oil. Cook the hare bonbons until golden, rolling them over to cook evenly on all sides, then serve hot with a fruity jelly alongside.

SUSSEX RESERVE

*This painting of Bridget's has become the symbol of Nutbourne Vineyards.
It depicts an old vine, dormant through the winter before it bursts back to life in the
springtime. This image has been featured on the Nutbourne Sussex Reserve wine label
for the past 15 years – more than half a million bottles have been admired,
drunk and enjoyed in that time.*

RICHARD'S WINES TO SHARE AND PAIR
Cousin Rupert and the Russians

I am often likened to my cousin Rupert, except he is now a Frenchman and I am English. However, we look similar, we both like to party and both of us have made the hospitality industry a way of life.

Rupert has worked in some fabulous restaurants, including the infamous Le Cap Horn perched on the ski piste above Courchevel. It is a favourite haunt for celebrities and Russian oligarchs, who compete with one another to demonstrate their superior wealth. The wily owner boasts a fine wine list featuring vintage first-growth Bordeaux priced in the thousands of euros. Rupert's role was to sell these wines. He did so with surprising regularity, but, more often than not, the 'special guests' would order a Coke alongside and then mix the two in the glass. Sadly, this is where the reputed finest wines in the world end up – completely wasted.

Don't worry, I am not going to recommend that you drink Chateau Latour or Lafite-Rothschild with the Steak & Oyster Pie. If you are in that bracket, good luck to you, you don't need my guidance. My recommendation is to go with something big and punchy – southern French reds such as Corbières, Ventoux or Languedoc.

STEAK & OYSTER PIE

In Dickensian England, steak and oyster pie was a poor household's staple. Oysters were plentiful, cheap and a good source of nourishment: the tighter the budget, the more oysters to beef in the pie. Of course, both of these ingredients are now considered a luxury, but the result of slow-cooked beef braised in a smoky wood-fired oven with the succulent tang of oysters and the rich suet crust makes something very special.

SERVES 6–8

For the beef filling

2–3 tbsp rapeseed oil

1kg chuck stewing steak, diced into 2.5cm cubes

100g plain flour

salt and freshly ground black pepper

1 large onion, sliced

2 carrots, peeled and sliced

2 garlic cloves, sliced

2 bay leaves

a few sprigs of thyme

600ml pale ale

2 tbsp Worcestershire sauce

1 tbsp English mustard

6–12 oysters, shucked

For the suet pastry

300g plain flour, plus extra for dusting

100g shredded suet

100g salted butter, chilled, plus extra for greasing

1 egg, lightly beaten

1 Make the beef filling. Heat 1 tbsp oil in a heavy-based casserole dish over a moderate heat. Roll the beef in seasoned flour, fry it in small batches until brown on all sides. Lift out the beef cubes with a slotted spoon and keep on the side.

2 Add another 1 tbsp oil to the casserole. Cook the onion and carrot until lightly browned. Stir in the garlic, bay and thyme, add the ale and bring to the boil.

3 Return the fried beef cubes to the casserole. Add the Worcestershire sauce and mustard, season well with salt and pepper. Put a lid or foil on the casserole, place it in a preheated low oven at 150°C to cook for 3 hours. Check the meat: it should be very tender but not dry.

4 Meanwhile, make the suet pastry. Put the flour and suet into a mixing bowl, grate the butter over. Using your fingers and thumbs, work the mixture together until it resembles coarse breadcrumbs. Add the egg and a few drops of cold water a little at a time, and work it into the mixture until you have a rough dough. Don't overwork the pastry, or it will become tough.

5 Form the pastry into a ball, wrap it in cling film and rest it in the fridge for at least an hour.

6 When the beef filling has finished cooking, remove it from the oven and increase the oven temperature to 180°C. Ladle the filling into a deep pie dish; add the shucked oysters, distributing them evenly throughout.

7 On a floured surface, roll out the pastry to a 1cm thick, even round, just a bit bigger than the rim of the pie dish. Butter the edge of the dish and place the pastry across the top, then trim any excess and neatly crimp the edges. Decorate the centre of the pie crust with an oyster shell.

8 Bake the pie in the oven for 40 minutes until the pastry is golden brown. Serve straight away with some nice winter vegetables and mashed potatoes.

TOFFEE GINGER PUDDING, RHUBARB & ORANGE

SERVES 8

oil, for greasing

100g dried dates, stoned and finely chopped

1 tsp bicarbonate of soda

175ml boiling water

80g butter, softened

140g caster sugar

2 eggs, beaten

165g self-raising flour

1 tsp ground ginger

60g stem ginger, finely chopped

For the toffee sauce

200g granulated sugar

50ml stem ginger syrup

100g butter, diced

120ml double cream

For the rhubarb

4 or 5 long stalks of pink rhubarb, washed and cut into 4cm lengths

2 tbsp water

100g caster sugar

1 orange, zest and juice

2 oranges, peel and pith removed, segmented

There are some classic puddings we never tire of. Sticky toffee can be adapted to include different flavours such as vanilla, chocolate or ginger – but at the end of the day, it remains a yummy northern British pudding with a reputation that has spread across the world. Forced rhubarb is a lovely vegetable but it has an unfortunate name. Basically, rhubarb is our best home-grown winter ingredient for fruity puddings and pies. 'Forcing' is the technique of covering the plant with a large pot or dark shelter so that it grows sweet, pink and tender in the coldest months of the year.

1 Preheat the oven to 180°C. Lightly oil a 20cm savarin ring mould.

2 Place the dates in a bowl with the bicarbonate of soda, then add the boiling water; set aside to soften.

3 Meanwhile, put the butter and sugar into the bowl of a stand mixer and whisk together until light and fluffy. While continuing to whisk, slowly add the eggs and flour, a little at a time, so the mixture doesn't curdle. Once fully mixed, fold in the ground ginger, stem ginger and the softened dates, including all the marinating juice.

4 Mix well, then spoon the mixture into the prepared ring mould and bake in the oven for 35 minutes, until firm to the touch. Turn it out on to a wire rack and leave to cool.

5 To prepare the toffee sauce, place the sugar in a heavy-based pan over a gentle heat, bring it to the boil and allow to bubble and caramelize. Once it has an even gold colour, take the pan off the heat. Mix the ginger syrup with a little water and add this to the pan. Stand back, as the mixture will spit. Stir and, if there are any sugar crystals, return the pan to a gentle heat until fully dissolved.

6 Stir in the butter, allow it to melt, then stir in the cream. Keep the sauce warm or chill it and reheat when required.

7 Prepare the rhubarb. Place the rhubarb, water, sugar and the zest and juice of one orange in a heavy-based pan over a gentle heat. Bring the mixture up to boil, then reduce the heat and simmer for 10–12 minutes, until the rhubarb is cooked through but still firm.

8 Allow the rhubarb to cool, then mix in the orange segments.

9 To serve, warm the toffee ginger pudding in a low oven, reheat the toffee sauce in a small pan, then fill the pudding with the rhubarb and orange. Lashings of custard would be good served alongside!

ESPRESSO MOCHA CHEESECAKE

I always think there is some significance to the last recipe in a cookbook. Perhaps it is because I am left-handed and therefore flick through a book from back to front – so the last recipe is the first for me! Anyway, there has been much debate between Bridget and me about this traditional, baked cheesecake. I want something light and risen but with a strong coffee-mocha flavour. Bridget is a much better baker than I, so after a few experiments, this is what we have come up with.

SERVES 8–10

For the base
150g digestive biscuits
75g butter
2 tbsp soft brown sugar
oil, for greasing

For the filling
4 eggs, separated
150g caster sugar
250g cream cheese
250g ricotta
1 tbsp self-raising flour
3 shots of strong espresso coffee

To finish
50g dark chocolate, grated
50g white chocolate, grated
cocoa powder, for dusting

1 Preheat the oven to 160°C. Line a 22cm springform cake tin with oiled baking paper.

2 Crush the biscuits by putting them in a plastic bag and bashing them with a wooden spoon. Melt the butter in a small pan over a low heat. In a bowl, combine the biscuits, melted butter and brown sugar.

3 Layer the biscuit mixture evenly across the base of the prepared cake tin, pressing it firmly into place. Chill it in the fridge while you make the filling.

4 Using a stand mixer, whisk the egg yolks and caster sugar together until pale and fluffy. Continue to whisk while adding the cream cheese, ricotta and flour. Pour in the espresso coffee and fold this into the cheese mixture.

5 In a separate bowl, whisk the egg whites until stiff but not too dry. Use a metal spoon to fold the egg whites through the cheese mixture.

6 Spoon the filling into the cake tin and smooth out the top. Bake in the oven for 1 hour. After this, turn off the oven and allow the cheesecake to cool inside, with the door still closed.

7 While the cake is cooking, make some chocolate lattice to decorate. Melt the dark and white chocolates separately in small bowls over saucepans of simmering water. Put a sheet of baking paper over a rolling pin and carefully drizzle the two melted chocolates over the curved paper to create lattice patterns. Leave to set.

8 Transfer the cheesecake to the fridge, to chill – but return to room temperature before serving.

9 To serve, remove the cake from the springform tin, peel off the baking paper, and place it on a serving dish. Use a small sieve to sprinkle cocoa powder over the top and decorate with the chocolate lattice.

ABOUT THE AUTHOR

Peter has published six books on the subject of cookery and entertainment. He has created and written this book on behalf of his whole family to celebrate their English vineyard.

The majority of Peter's working life has been spent as a chef and business owner in the hospitality sector. He started his own private catering business (Party Ingredients Catering Services Ltd) in 1975 and then the Gladwin Restaurant Group from 1993 onwards. He and his family live in West Sussex, where they farm and are the proprietors of Nutbourne Vineyards – producers of award-winning English still and sparkling wine. The family businesses encompassing restaurants, farming and wine all share the concept 'Local & Wild', a way of life and commitment to provenance, people and the countryside.

Peter has served as Chairman of the United Kingdom Vineyards Association and then Vice-Chairman of Wines of Great Britain. He is now Honorary Vice-President of Wines of Great Britain. In acknowledgement of his work in the City of London, Peter has been made a Liveryman of the Drapers' Company and Honorary Freeman of the Apothecaries', Clothworkers', Launderers' and Saddlers' livery companies.

Peter has published six books on the subject of cookery and entertainment. During the Covid-19 Pandemic he worked with City Livery Companies to set up the Livery Kitchen Initiative providing meals for NHS workers and community projects in deprived areas of London. He also wrote the associated *Livery Kitchen Cookbook*.

Peter now concentrates on his wine production in Sussex, as well as writing and speaking on the topics of cookery, healthy eating, wine and food sustainability.

CITY HARVEST CHARITY

Food poverty is a huge and growing issue in the UK with over 5.7 million families skipping meals because they cannot afford to eat. The Gladwin Family are aware that our vineyard, wines and restaurants are for a privileged section of society and we acknowledge our good fortune. Therefore, all royalties from this publication are being donated to an organization called City Harvest.

City Harvest is a charity that rescues wasted or unwanted food and redistributes it to those who really need it through 375 charities and community projects throughout London. All the food is donated and the charity charges nothing to those who receive it. This work saves surplus food, feeds hungry people and reduces pollution from wastage. To learn more about this great organization, visit its website: cityharvest.org.uk.

INDEX

For Bridget – wife, artist, vigneron and mother who has made Nutbourne the very special place that it is.

PUBLISHER Jonathan Bailey
PRODUCTION Jim Bulley
SENIOR PROJECT EDITOR Susie Behar
EDITOR Susie Johns
DESIGNER Michael Whitehead
FOOD PRODUCTION Oliver Gladwin, Bridget Gladwin & Emma Spofforth
PHOTOGRAPHY Ed Dallimore
PHOTOGRAPHY EDITING Olivia Thomas
COLOUR ORIGINATION GMC Reprographics

Printed and bound in China

CONVERSION CHART

GAS MARK	FAHRENHEIT	CELSIUS	FAN
1	275	140	120
2	300	150	130
3	325	160	140
4	350	180	160
5	375	190	170
6	400	200	180
7	425	220	200

All oven temperatures in this book are for fan-assisted electric ovens.

To order a book, contact:
GMC Publications Ltd
Castle Place, 166 High Street,
Lewes, East Sussex, BN7 1XU
United Kingdom
Tel: +44 (0)1273 488005
www.gmcbooks.com

Note
Unless specified, butter can be salted or unsalted.